SUCCESS!

SUCCESS!

CHARACTER STUDIES FROM THE BIBLE

EVERETT LEADINGHAM, EDITOR

Though this book is designed for group study,
it is also intended for personal enjoyment and
spiritual growth. A leader's guide is available from
your local bookstore or your publisher.

Beacon Hill Press of Kansas City
Kansas City, Missouri

Editor: Everett Leadingham
Associate Editor: Charlie L. Yourdon
Executive Editor: Randy Cloud
Editorial Committee: Philip Baisley, Randy Cloud, Everett Leadingham,
Tom Mayse, Larry Morris, Blaine A. Smith, Darlene Teague, Richard
Willowby, Mark York, Charlie Yourdon

Cover design: Paul Franitza

10   9   8   7   6   5   4   3   2   1

Contents

1. The Picture of Success (Abraham)   6
   by C. S. Cowles

2. Success and Power (Joseph and Saul)   16
   by Frank Moore

3. Success and Self-Esteem (Moses, Jeremiah, Gideon)   26
   by David Thompson

4. Success and Public Opinion (Joshua and Caleb)   36
   by Lonni Collins Pratt

5. Success and Self-Interest (Ruth and Esther)   44
   by Melanie Starks Kierstead

6. Success, I Deserve It! (Job)   54
   by Richard K. Eckley

7. The Source of Success (Isaiah)   64
   by John N. Oswalt

8. The Price of Success   72
   (The Rich Young Ruler and Paul)
   by Carl M. Leth

9. The Measure of Success (The Widow and Mary)   80
   by Stephen Lennox

10. Success and Failure (Peter and Judas)   88
    by Gaymon Bennett

11. All the Right Moves (Daniel)   98
    by Gene Van Note

12. All the Right Reasons (John the Baptist)   108
    by Donald Demaray

13. All or Nothing (Jesus and Solomon)   118
    by H. Ray Dunning

THE WORLD'S VIEW

Success comes from working a plan.

THE BIBLE'S VIEW

Success results from following a Person.

Abraham

By faith Abraham, when called to go to a place he would later receive as his inheritance, obeyed and went, even though he did not know where he was going. By faith he made his home in the promised land like a stranger in a foreign country; he lived in tents, as did Isaac and Jacob, who were heirs with him of the same promise. For he was looking forward to the city with foundations, whose architect and builder is God.

By faith Abraham, even though he was past age—and Sarah herself was barren—was enabled to become a father because he considered him faithful who had made the promise. And so from this one man, and he as good as dead, came descendants as numerous as the stars in the sky and as countless as the sand on the seashore.

All these people were still living by faith when they died. They did not receive the things promised; they only saw them and welcomed them from a distance. And they admitted that they were aliens and strangers on earth. People who say such things show that they are looking for a country of their own. If they had been thinking of the country they had left, they would have had opportunity to return. Instead, they were longing for a better country—a heavenly one. Therefore God is not ashamed to be called their God, for he has prepared a city for them.

By faith Abraham, when God tested him, offered Isaac as a sacrifice. He who had received the promises was about to sacrifice his one and only son, even though God had said to him, "It is through Isaac that your offspring will be reckoned." Abraham reasoned that God could raise the dead, and figuratively speaking, he did receive Isaac back from death (Hebrews 11:8-19).

1
THE PICTURE
OF SUCCESS

by C. S. Cowles

Abraham? A picture of success? On the surface there's little to suggest it.

In his novel *The Plague,* Albert Camus devotes a short paragraph to profiling Joseph Grand. The only "grand" thing about him, however, is his name. Camus summarizes him in this way: "In short, Joseph Grand had all the attributes of insignificance."[1]

Could not the same be said of Abraham? He was, after all, a "dropout" from the ancient "cradle of civilization," the intellectual and cultural center of his world. A wandering, homeless exile in a foreign land. One who looked for a city but who lived and died in a tent.

Abraham led no mighty armies, governed no great nation, and wrote no books. He did none of the things by which we measure greatness. Not once, but twice, he palmed off his wife as his sister in order to save his own skin. Impatient for the heir God had promised, he sired a son by his wife's Egyptian slave woman. To keep Sarah happy after Isaac was born, he expelled Hagar, and Ishmael—his own flesh and blood—from his house and home. He drove them off into a trackless wilderness where they would have died had they not been rescued by God.

Which raises an intriguing question: How did Abraham, who like Joseph Grand had all the "attributes of insignificance," become such a dominant figure in Scripture, a patriarch of the greatest significance? Abraham looms so large that 12 chapters in Genesis are devoted to telling his story—"warts and all." Besides that, he is mentioned another 42 times in the Old Testament and an astonishing 72 times in the New Testament. Paul devotes more attention to Abraham than Moses, David, and all other Old Testament personalities put together. Abraham becomes, for Paul, the prime example of salvation by grace through faith (see Romans 4; Galatians 3:6-18).

What was Abraham's secret? Why is it important that we study him in order to gain an idea of how the Bible regards success? What were the qualities of character he exhibited that we should strive to have?

Abraham Was a Dreamer

"Here comes that dreamer!" (Genesis 37:19), said the sons of Jacob about their brother Joseph. That could very well have been said of Abraham, Joseph's great-grandfather, and the most daring dreamer of all. Abraham did not, however, spin dreams out of thin air. Rather they were ignited in his mind, heart, and soul by a surprising call of God that was as scary as it was exhilarating: "Leave your country, your people and your father's household and go to the land I will show you" (12:1).

God's call included a mind-boggling promise: "I will make you into a great nation and I will bless you; I will make your name great, and you will be a blessing. . . . and all peoples on earth will be blessed through you" (vv. 2-3).

Abraham embraced and internalized this astonishing revelation so completely that God's call became his vision and his vocation. Unlike contemporary titans of the political, corporate, and entertainment worlds, Abraham did not dream of prestige, power, and prosperity. However, he was, by the standards of his day, a man of considerable wealth, a fact that was not a handicap but a help in the fulfillment of God's plans for his life. Even as mountain climbers become smitten with "summit fever," so Abraham lived for the heights. Like his forefather Enoch, Abraham "walked with God" (5:22). He dreamed of that which was solid, that which was grounded, not in the uncertainties of this present world but in God, in what would far outlast his brief sojourn on earth. To see himself as the one through whom "all peoples on earth will be blessed" (12:3)—including yet unborn generations —constitutes an expansive order of dreaming almost beyond comprehension.

Which raises the question: What is the shape, texture, and breadth of our vision? "Where there is no vision, the people perish" (Proverbs 29:18, KJV).

Abraham Was a "Countercultural Revolutionary"

Abraham had an understanding of God that was different from—even in direct conflict with—the polytheistic worldview of his day. God revealed himself as one, not many; as a holy, compassionate Lord over all; as one who initiated covenant relationships with human beings.

Abraham broke with the corrupt and immoral religious and cultural world of his day and struck out on his own. In so doing, God revealed a radical new understanding of time to Abraham and his prophetic heirs. Time goes in a straight line, not in a circle, an eternal cycle, like the cycle of seasons, where there can be neither a real history nor a genuine future. "In the *beginning* God created the heavens and the earth" (Genesis 1:1, emphasis added). Time has a beginning, moves ever forward in successive stages, and is irrevocably drawn toward a future that is as open as God and as boundless as eternity. Consequently, every new day is a new creation—a day of opportunity, discovery, and destiny. The tyranny of the past is broken. Everything is possible, and all things become new.

Which raises the question: How countercultural are we? Are we, like Jesus, "not of the world" (John 17:16)? "Do not conform any longer to the pattern of this world," said Paul, "but be transformed by the renewing of your mind" (Romans 12:2).

Abraham Was Daring

At every stage along his spiritual journey, he responded to God's leadership with radical obedience. When God called, he launched out into the deep, "even though he did not know where he was going" (Hebrews 11:8). Whenever God spoke, he answered. Whatever God commanded, he did. All that God promised, he believed.

Nowhere is Abraham's radical obedience more evident than when God asked him to offer up his son Isaac as a sacrifice. What was extraordinary about this test of faith was that Isaac was a miracle baby, a marvelous gift of God himself. Now God was asking him to relinquish his son—his only son—and the only means by which God's sweeping promise of "a great nation" (Genesis 12:2) could be fulfilled. One can only speculate how much intense spiritual agony this caused Abraham. Nevertheless, once again he obeyed God.

I have seen that kind of radical obedience firsthand. My father spent the difficult years of the Great Depression carving out a newspaper and printing business while also serving as a bivocational pastor. Right after the close of World War II, he received a letter from a mission director in Hong Kong inviting him to come and serve as a "faith missionary." He immediately sent his answer by return mail: "We're coming, just as soon as I can sell my business." Mother was surprised but also delighted by father's impulsive decision. She had dreamed with him, for years, of going as missionaries to the land where he had been raised, the son of pioneer missionaries.

That my two brothers, my sister, and I are still alive—and all serving Christ—is testimony to God's faithfulness in providing for those who have no better sense than to answer God's call with an immediate "Here am I. Send me!" (Isaiah 6:8). My wife and I had the joy of watching our oldest son and his wife respond to God's call to invest two years of their life in Kenya as medical missionaries like my parents—without salary. They look back on that experience of radical obedience as the most exciting and spiritually rewarding time of their lives.

Which raises the question: When God calls, are we ready, like Abraham and Jesus' disciples, to "launch out into the deep" (Luke 5:4, KJV)? "Whoever loses his life for me and for the gospel," said Jesus, "will save it" (Mark 8:35).

Abraham Was Selfless

When the land could not support both his and Lot's "flocks and herds and tents" (Genesis 13:5), Abraham suggested that

they "part company" amicably (v. 9). Though Abraham had the
right to the land that was "well watered, like the garden of
the LORD" (v. 10), he gave first choice to his nephew. Lot chose
the fertile "plain of the Jordan" (v. 11), even though the notori-
ously wicked cities of Sodom and Gomorrah were nearby. Later,
when God revealed that Sodom and Gomorrah were going to be
destroyed, Abraham passionately interceded with God for the
lives of Lot and his family. Abraham would not argue, much less
bargain, with God for himself, yet he would stretch to the limit
on behalf of others.

Which raises the question: How generous are we in looking
"not only to your own interests, but also to the interests of others" (Philippians 2:4)? "For even the Son of Man did not come to
be served, but to serve, and to give his life as a ransom for many"
(Mark 10:45).

Abraham Exercised Extraordinary Faith

Abraham stands as the towering example in Hebrews's roll
call of faith. His was a *saving* faith: "Abram believed the LORD, and
he credited it to him as righteousness" (Genesis 15:6). His was a
venturing faith. "When called to go to a place he would later receive as his inheritance," Abraham obeyed, "even though he did
not know where he was going" (Hebrews 11:8). His was an *accept-
ing* faith. Though he was "a stranger in a foreign country," he
adopted it as his homeland because God had promised it to him
(v. 9). His was a *visionary* faith. "For he was looking forward to the
city with foundations, whose architect and builder is God" (v. 10).

Most importantly, Abraham exercised *resurrection* faith. Even
though Sarah was barren and he himself was "as good as dead,"
he "considered him faithful who had made the promise" of a son
(vv. 11-12). He believed that God could bring life out of death.
When Abraham saw in the distance the place where he was to
sacrifice Isaac, he said to his servants, "Stay here with the donkey
while I and the boy go over there. We will worship and then *we
will come back* to you" (Genesis 22:5, emphasis added). He never
doubted that God would intervene to save Isaac's life or would

raise him from the dead. Either way Abraham knew that God could be trusted to keep His promise of giving him "descendants as numerous as the stars in the sky and as countless as the sand on the seashore" (Hebrews 11:12). When we consider that there are 1.6 billion Christians today, it is clear that God keeps His promises.

We come back to Joseph Grand. Though he was a minor character in Camus's story, in the end he became a person of great significance. Grand was infected with the bubonic plague virus, like tens of thousands of others in the blighted city of Oran, and became critically ill. Yet unlike all before him, he did not die. His "resurrection" from the illness signaled that the back of the plague had been broken. Life triumphed over death, and hope over despair. The city was delivered, and a new day dawned.

So it was with Abraham. His obedience anticipated his heir, Jesus of Nazareth, who was "obedient to death—even death on a cross!" (Philippians 2:8). Abraham's resurrection faith was vindicated when God raised Jesus from the dead. His confidence that God would make his "name great" (Genesis 12:2) is being fulfilled wherever God is exalting Jesus as Lord (Philippians 2:9); for wherever the name of Jesus goes, there the name of Abraham goes as well. His rock-solid faith that through him "all peoples on earth will be blessed" (Genesis 12:3) is even now being realized wherever people turn from darkness to light, and will finally be consummated when "every knee [shall] bow . . . and every tongue confess that Jesus Christ is Lord, to the glory of God the Father" (Philippians 2:10-11).

Father Arseny, a Russian Orthodox priest who spent nearly 20 years in the black hole of Stalin's dreaded Siberian slave-labor death camps, embodied Abraham's spiritual characteristics. Though condemned to being "in the world" of bottomless misery, cruelty, and despair, he was "not of the world." He was always willing to share his meager rations with men who were sick or whose food had been stolen by criminals, and was constantly looking for ways to help his fellow prisoners. He exercised radical obedience by refusing to sign a false confession that would have indicted fellow prisoners in a plot against Stalin. For that selfless act, he was beaten unconscious.

What surviving prisoners remembered most about Father Arseny was his undaunted faith in God. He became known as the "old man who prayed all the time." Through unceasing prayer, he was able to rise above the degradation, debauchery, and savagery going on all around him. Often he would spend the night caring for and praying over a sick or injured man or stand by his bunk praying quietly all night. The prisoners could not understand how he kept going and still managed to work so hard with so little food and sleep. Through prayer, he entered into another world. He seemed to tap into invisible sources of nourishment and rest that amazed everyone, even the guards.

For intervening in stopping a new prisoner, Alexei, from being beaten to death by criminals, Father Arseny and the young man whose life he saved were condemned to spend 48 hours in an unheated concrete and iron punishment cell. Two former atheists, who had become believers, begged the camp supervisor not to do it in that there was no way they could survive in the minus 22 degree weather, especially since they were not permitted to take coats or blankets. Still, the sentence was imposed. Alexei, also suffering from the beating he had received, began to shiver uncontrollably. His feet, legs, and arms were fast becoming numb as the freezing cold moved up his limbs. Father Arseny told him to lie down and rest and he would pray for him. Giving up hope, Alexei lay down to die. Yet he could not help but listen to the priest's words as he now fervently prayed aloud.

As Alexei watched the praying priest, suddenly things began to change. A bright light flooded the cell. The walls seemed to widen. Alarmed, Alexei thought he was either dying or losing his mind. Father Arseny was now clothed in brilliant white vestments, lifting his hands in prayer before the altar of a church. Two men, with radiant faces and dressed in glowing vestments, assisted the priest as he sang psalms, performed the liturgy, and prayed. The death cell became a warm and beautiful house of worship. Alexei found himself praying right along with the priest.

He was not repeating the words *after* the priest, rather he was praying *simultaneously* with him. Somehow he knew exactly what to say. An incredible sense of joy and peace washed over him as the glory of God filled his soul.

When the supervisor and guards opened the punishment cell door two days later, they jumped back in fright. They had expected to haul out two frozen cadavers. Instead, they found the prisoners, with eyes bright, faces glowing, clothed in pure white garments. Actually, it was hoarfrost that covered them.

Alexei, an atheist, became an Orthodox priest upon his release. Scores of prisoners subsequently became believers in Jesus Christ. Father Arseny was one of the few to survive for such a long time—two decades—in a death camp. Though forbidden to serve a church upon his release, he exercised a vast ministry among his spiritual children, as well as countless others who had been deeply impacted by his extraordinary life. People flocked to his tiny boardinghouse room, many traveling hundreds of miles, in order to receive his counsel, instruction, and prayers for them. Many were added to Christ's kingdom through his long and faithful life of ministry.

Father Arseny died in 1973 at 80 years of age. Yet his influence, and that of countless others like him, lives on in spiritual "descendants as numerous as the stars in the sky and as countless as the sand on the seashore" (Hebrews 11:12).[2]

Notes

1. Albert Camus, *The Plague* (New York: Random House, 1948), 42.

2. Vera Bouteneff, trans., *Father Arseny 1893—1973: Priest, Prisoner, Spiritual Father* (Crestwood, N.Y.: St. Vladimier's Seminary Press, 1999), 33-37.

About the Author: Dr. Cowles is professor of biblical literature and preaching at Northwest Nazarene University, Nampa, Idaho.

THE WORLD'S VIEW

Success is having power over people for personal gain.

THE BIBLE'S VIEW

Success is using God's gift of power to serve Him and those He has given us the responsibility to serve.

Joseph

So Joseph went after his brothers and found them near Dothan. But they saw him in the distance, and before he reached them, they plotted to kill him.

"Here comes that dreamer!" they said to each other. "Come now, let's kill him and throw him into one of these cisterns and say that a ferocious animal devoured him. Then we'll see what comes of his dreams."

When Reuben heard this, he tried to rescue him from their hands. "Let's not take his life," he said. "Don't shed any blood. Throw him into this cistern here in the desert, but don't lay a hand on him." Reuben said this to rescue him from them and take him back to his father.

So when Joseph came to his brothers, they stripped him of his robe—the richly ornamented robe he was wearing—and they took him and threw him into the cistern. Now the cistern was empty; there was no water in it.

As they sat down to eat their meal, they looked up and saw a caravan of Ishmaelites coming from Gilead. Their camels were loaded with spices, balm and myrrh, and they were on their way to take them down to Egypt.

Judah said to his brothers, "What will we gain if we kill our brother and cover up his blood? Come, let's sell him to the Ishmaelites and not lay our hands on him; after all, he is our brother, our own flesh and blood." His brothers agreed.

So when the Midianite merchants came by, his brothers pulled Joseph up out of the cistern and sold him for twenty shekels of silver to the Ishmaelites, who took him to Egypt (Genesis 37:17-28).

Saul

Now the Philistines fought against Israel; the Israelites fled before them, and many fell slain on Mount Gilboa. The Philistines pressed hard after Saul and his sons, and they killed his sons Jonathan, Abinadab and Malki-Shua. The fighting grew fierce around Saul, and when the archers overtook him, they wounded him critically.

Saul said to his armor-bearer, "Draw your sword and run me through, or these uncircumcised fellows will come and run me through and abuse me."

But his armor-bearer was terrified and would not do it; so Saul took his own sword and fell on it. When the armor-bearer saw that Saul was dead, he too fell on his sword and died with him. So Saul and his three sons and his armor-bearer and all his men died together that same day (1 Samuel 31:1-6).

2
SUCCESS
AND POWER

by Frank Moore

The citizens of Egypt stood around television sets in homes, restaurants, offices, and electronics stores throughout the country. The big day had arrived; Pharaoh's installation of the new prime minister was taking place in the national palace. Television cameras and floodlights filled the throne room. News reporters from around the world packed the official newsroom as they prepared reports for home. Trumpets sounded; the ceremony began. Pharaoh and his entire court entered the throne room and took their respective places of honor. A young man stepped from a side room and took his place in front of Pharaoh. The young man knelt in respective honor before the most powerful man in the kingdom. The crowd watched with bated breath.

Pharaoh lifted the young man's hand as he stood straight. Pharaoh placed a signet ring on the young man's finger, a gold necklace around his neck, and a cloak of fine linen across his shoulders. Pharaoh pronounced the words of induction. The ceremony proceeded as representatives from every branch of government pledged their support to the new prime minister. After an hour of pomp and circumstance, the induction ceremony ended. The civil officials, dignitaries, and honored guests retired to a reception in the adjoining banquet hall. Pharaoh spared no expense on this special day of celebration. Television reporters returned viewers to the anchor desk for an analysis of the day's events.

News anchors began to examine the life and background of their new prime minister. One news piece after another probed interesting questions. Who was this Joseph? Where did he come

from? What was his family like? What circumstances influenced his life to bring him to this place of special honor—second in command of the most powerful nation in the world? As we watch this day's events, we can't help but feel a little envious of today's star. Why did this 30-year-old man get such a big break? Why couldn't we have had the privileges he enjoyed? How did he climb to the top of the political ladder so quickly? What was the secret of his success? Why so much power for so young a man? A hundred other questions flood our minds as we listen to the news reports and contemplate the honors of this day—all focused on one hero.

A Disastrous Homelife

The true picture is not at all like it might first appear. Joseph had no favored life, at least not the way we usually think of "favored." His early years weren't charmed, by any stretch of the imagination. Born into a dysfunctional family, Joseph grew up the hard way with a great deal of domestic tension and strife. His father Jacob fled from his parents' homeland long before Joseph was born. He'd heard the stories though, stories about lies and deception between Jacob's mother and father that finally ended with the young man fleeing the country. The stories also spun a tale of Jacob's estranged brother Esau who had once threatened to kill Jacob the next time they met.

The situation with Joseph's grandparents on his mother's side of the family wasn't any better. More deception and lies. Another move from the extended family to get away from tension and strife.

Matters under Jacob's roof weren't any better. Jacob fathered children with four different women, all living under the same roof. Not a very happy camp much of the time! To make matters worse, Jacob told everyone that one of these four women, Rachel (Joseph's mother), was his favorite. That "honor" didn't help Joseph with 10 of his brothers. Joseph was "Daddy's boy," and his brothers hated him for it. Joseph's mother died when he was young, as she gave birth to his brother Benjamin. This endeared Rachel's 2 boys even more closely to their father's heart. Every time Jacob looked into these sons' eyes, he saw his beloved Rachel.

Joseph's 10 brothers might have endured the situation, if their father hadn't constantly reminded them of Joseph's favored status. The multicolored coat symbolized this special father-son relationship. Yet, Joseph pushed his brothers' patience over the edge when he naively—or maybe not so naively—told them about his dreams of them bowing before him. They'd felt like killing him for years; now, they were ready to do it—literally. If it hadn't been for Joseph's brother Reuben, they probably would have too.

So, did Joseph have a favored home environment? No. He spent the first 17 years of his life living in a home with a great deal of domestic tension, estranged from his extended family, hated by his brothers, suffering from the loss of his mother, and doted over by his biased father. Not exactly a formula for success.

The Dream Turned into a Nightmare

As the inauguration day news reports on Joseph's early life continue, it's hard to believe the strange turn the story takes. The angry, jealous brothers plotted his death. Then they dumped him in an empty water cistern, where many people died in those days. No doubt Joseph sat in the underground darkness, imagining the worst. His life flashed before his eyes. What good did it do him to be "Daddy's boy" now? It didn't look like his brothers would be bowing before him anytime soon! His dreams must have been nothing more than a fanciful imagination run wild or the effects of a spicy meal.

The cistern lid eventually opened and flooded Joseph's dungeon with sunlight and noise of businessmen striking deals. The brothers hoisted young Joseph out of the hole and onto the back of a camel headed toward Egypt. "Why kill the little smart aleck when we can sell him as a slave?" the brothers conspired. "That ought to take care of 'Daddy's dreamer boy'!" This turn of events is not exactly the standard formula for building a successful life.

From Bad to Worse

Things didn't get any better for Joseph in Egypt. He found himself standing exposed on an auction block, with the highest bidder taking him as a slave. He brought a good price, no doubt, because he was strong and handsome. Yet, he would soon wish he were not so desirable. His new owner, Potiphar, trusted him so much that Joseph had everything that belonged to Potiphar at his disposal except for one person—Potiphar's wife.

Despite Joseph's personal integrity, Mrs. Potiphar tried every trick in her arsenal to seduce young Joseph into her carnal clutches. All of her female weapons remained powerless to break his spiritual resolve and commitment to God. She punished his continual rejection by falsely accusing him of the very adultery he refused to commit. Unfortunately, Potiphar believed the web of lies his wife spun about Joseph, and the young Hebrew found himself in prison.

It's not supposed to happen like that! Good things should result from staying true to God's commands. Not always. Joseph found that, not only do young men of integrity sometimes find themselves in a hole in the ground and in a foreign land on a slave's auction block, they also can end up imprisoned for no just reason. As far as Joseph knew, the childhood dream he shared with his older brothers was as good as dead. Again, this story is not exactly the standard formula for building a successful life.

Behind Bars

Several news reports follow, documenting the ups and downs of Joseph's continued bad fortune while in jail. Time does not permit a detailed analysis of each one. Suffice it to say they didn't paint a pleasant picture. However, the Lord didn't let Joseph go to prison alone. He stood beside him during these bewildering years and even blessed him. It wasn't just personal, spiritual blessings, either. Even the prison warden and the other prisoners realized that the Lord was with Joseph. In time, he rose to a place of power again—in prison. You just can't keep a good man down, even when he's behind bars for a crime he didn't commit. He helped fellow inmates and prison officials and did all sorts of good deeds while serving his sentence.

It occasionally looked like he might secure his release, but again and again the tables turned on him, and he stayed right where injustice placed him. If Joseph hadn't had bad luck during this period of his life, he wouldn't have had any luck at all! Still, he didn't let his adversity sour his spirit and attitude. He talked to the Lord throughout the day, and the Lord instructed him in His own personal way. Prison—not exactly the standard formula for building a successful life.

Cream Rises

One final news report on this special inauguration day highlights the unusual turn of events that ended Joseph's 13-year prison term. God warned Pharaoh in a dream that a famine would soon descend on Egypt. Pharaoh heeded the warning and prepared his country for a regional disaster. He needed someone to spearhead the national campaign for preparation and conducted a nationwide search for a wise, sensitive leader who evidenced the Spirit of God in his life. The search led them straight to Joseph's prison cell! Joseph received an immediate pardon. Pharaoh's court planned an inauguration ceremony to install him as second in command of the most powerful nation in the world.

As the televised coverage of the events of this momentous day come to a close and the television stations return to normal programming, we can't help but feel a little confused. All of the reports had a common theme: the star of the day didn't exactly illustrate the standard formula for building a successful life. He didn't even offer an example that many people would want to follow. He did, however, illustrate an important truth—cream always rises.

Joseph remained faithful to God through all of the adversities and misfortunes of his life. He left the timing of his life in the hands of God. In His own unique way, God promoted Joseph to a significant position of success and power. History reveals that Joseph learned his lessons well during the deep waters of his life. He was an outstanding leader throughout his reign in Egypt. Everything he did until his dying day reflected a spirit of godliness, humility, and highest character. In fact, Joseph received one of the best report cards of any Bible hero. A true pattern for our lives.

Life Lessons

So, what do we learn about success and power from the life of Joseph? Several things. First, he gives us no set formula for leadership development. You'd never read Joseph's testimony in a book titled *Making It to the Top in Six Easy Steps*. Even if someone dared write such a book, it wouldn't sell because few of us would want to be misunderstood, mistreated, misused, and abused the way Joseph was. Adversity, however, seems to have offered a very good training ground for him. Some lessons in life can only be learned at the bottom of a hole or in jail. That's never an easy thing to say, but it's true nonetheless.

We also learn something about God's companionship with those who rely on Him. Joseph is the only Hebrew Patriarch (a title given to Abraham, Isaac, Jacob, and Joseph as the original leaders of the Hebrew nation) who did not receive visitations directly from God. God appeared to Abraham seven times, to Isaac twice, and to Jacob five times. Joseph didn't even get one heavenly visitation while in the well or jail. Nobody knows why. Maybe his faith was strong without it. Maybe he lived close enough to God to see Him with spiritual eyes, so God didn't need to make a physical appearance.

Joseph also reminds us that the road to success requires things not always highly regarded by people these days. Things like obedience, honesty, goodness, godliness, kindness, purity, humility, patience, self-control, and selfless love often get high marks in casual conversation but take a backseat in the hard decisions of life. Joseph reminds us that these things eventually pay off, if we practice them faithfully and learn from them. He also reminds us that these virtues remain high in God's value system, even if the bottom falls out from under their stock in our secular society. Tell Hollywood to practice abstinence and purity; they'll laugh you out of the theater. Tell businesspeople to always tell the truth; they'll lie to your face. Tell your secular friends to turn the other cheek when misused at work; they may think you've lost your mind.

We're also reminded by Joseph to put our situation in God's hands and let Him control it. That's easier said than done. His movements are seldom visual enough for us. It's easy to forget the rock-solid fact—God is always doing more behind the scenes than we ever see on the surface. For some reason, God prefers to work quietly in the shadows of our uncertainty. Five times in Genesis 39 alone (vv. 2, 3, 5, 21, 23) we're told that God had His hand on Joseph. Joseph may not have known it at the time, but God continued to work in silence. That's actually a very important success principle: place your trust in Sovereign God to accomplish His purposes in your life, and continue to do what's right.

Joseph further illustrates that you can't always predict who's going to make a good leader. Few people would have seen much leadership potential in Joseph during his teen years. He was spoiled and arrogant. His brothers who knew him best wanted to kill him. No, if we were banking on futures, most of us would have bet on a young man like Saul (1 Samuel 8—15). He was tall, humble, and favored by all. He even ran from the ceremony when it came time to crown him king. God blessed his life, and everyone in the land recognized his incredible leadership ability.

Unfortunately something went terribly wrong in Saul's life. The success and power went to his head as he adopted a worldly view of success—living in luxury while exercising power over people for personal gain. The longer Saul lived, the more twisted his motives and actions became. He ultimately hit rock bottom. What a tragic waste of God's investment in his life!

Joseph, on the other hand, adopted a biblical view of success. He learned to humble himself before God, see every good thing that came his way as a gift from God, and find ways every day to serve others. Power to him meant servanthood. He remained humble throughout his life. What an incredible development of God's investment in his life!

Perhaps the best summary statement of Joseph's entire life came from his own mouth many years later once he was reunited with his brothers. While analyzing all the bad things they did to him, Joseph replied, "You intended to harm me, but God intended it for good to accomplish what is now being done, the saving of many lives" (Genesis 50:20).

About the Author: Dr. Moore is vice president for academic affairs at MidAmerica Nazarene University, Olathe, Kansas.

THE WORLD'S VIEW

Success begins with good self-esteem.

THE BIBLE'S VIEW

Success begins with proper God-esteem.

Moses

Now Moses was tending the flock of Jethro his father-in-law, the priest of Midian, and he led the flock to the far side of the desert and came to Horeb, the mountain of God. There the angel of the LORD appeared to him in flames of fire from within a bush. Moses saw that though the bush was on fire it did not burn up. So Moses thought, "I will go over and see this strange sight—why the bush does not burn up."

When the LORD saw that he had gone over to look, God called to him from within the bush, "Moses! Moses!"

And Moses said, "Here I am."

"Do not come any closer," God said. "Take off your sandals, for the place where you are standing is holy ground." Then he said, "I am the God of your father, the God of Abraham, the God of Isaac and the God of Jacob." At this, Moses hid his face, because he was afraid to look at God.

The LORD said, "I have indeed seen the misery of my people in Egypt. I have heard them crying out because of their slave drivers, and I am concerned about their suffering. So I have come down to rescue them from the hand of the Egyptians and to bring them up out of that land into a good and spacious land, a land flowing with milk and honey—the home of the Canaanites, Hittites, Amorites, Perizzites, Hivites and Jebusites. And now the cry of the Israelites has reached me, and I have seen the way the Egyptians are oppressing them. So now, go. I am sending you to Pharaoh to bring my people the Israelites out of Egypt."

But Moses said to God, "Who am I, that I should go to Pharaoh and bring the Israelites out of Egypt?"

And God said, "I will be with you. And this will be the sign to you that it is I who have sent you: When you have brought the people out of Egypt, you will worship God on this mountain" (Exodus 3:1-12).

Jeremiah

The word of the LORD came to me, saying,
"Before I formed you in the womb I knew you,
before you were born I set you apart;
I appointed you as a prophet to the nations."

"Ah, Sovereign LORD," I said, "I do not know how to speak; I am only a child."

But the LORD said to me, "Do not say, 'I am only a child.' You must go to everyone I send you to and say whatever I command you. Do not be afraid of them, for I am with you and will rescue you," declares the LORD.

Then the LORD reached out his hand and touched my mouth and said to me, "Now, I have put my words in your mouth. See, today I appoint you over nations and kingdoms to uproot and tear down, to destroy and overthrow, to build and to plant."

The word of the LORD came to me: "What do you see, Jeremiah?"

"I see the branch of an almond tree," I replied.

The LORD said to me, "You have seen correctly, for I am watching to see that my word is fulfilled."

The word of the LORD came to me again: "What do you see?"

"I see a boiling pot, tilting away from the north," I answered.

The LORD said to me, "From the north disaster will be poured out on all who live in the land. I am about to summon all the peoples of the northern kingdoms," declares the LORD. . . .

"Get yourself ready! Stand up and say to them whatever I command you. Do not be terrified by them, or I will terrify you before them. Today I have made you a fortified city, an iron pillar and a bronze wall to stand against the whole land—against the kings of Judah, its officials, its priests and the people of the land. They will fight against you but will not overcome you, for I am with you and will rescue you," declares the LORD (Jeremiah 1:4-15, 17-19).

Gideon

The angel of the LORD came and sat down under the oak in Ophrah that belonged to Joash the Abiezrite, where his son Gideon was threshing wheat in a winepress to keep it from the Midianites. When the angel of the LORD appeared to Gideon, he said, "The LORD is with you, mighty warrior."

"But sir," Gideon replied, "if the LORD is with us, why has all this happened to us? Where are all his wonders that our fathers told us about when they said, 'Did not the LORD bring us up out of Egypt?' But now the LORD has abandoned us and put us into the hand of Midian."

The LORD turned to him and said, "Go in the strength you have and save Israel out of Midian's hand. Am I not sending you?"

"But Lord," Gideon asked, "how can I save Israel? My clan is the weakest in Manasseh, and I am the least in my family."

The LORD answered, "I will be with you, and you will strike down all the Midianites together" (Judges 6:11-16).

3
SUCCESS AND SELF-ESTEEM

by David Thompson

The biblical characters Moses, Gideon, and Jeremiah present striking differences. Yet, they share one very obvious thing in common: the conviction that they were absolutely the wrong person for the job God wanted them to do! Even the short version of the story on each of them shows why they are case studies in success and self-esteem.

The self-esteem issues in these stories probably have more to do with understandable feelings of inadequacy than with damaged views of self-worth. God taps persons for "impossible" assignments, demanding resources beyond their own. Still, they might as well be persons scarred by abuse or abandonment of various sorts. Whatever the source of their "I can't do it" response, the results will be similar. The mission will not be accomplished without some breakthrough insight and enabling.

Moses: Surely Not Me!

Exodus 3:1—4:17 carries the prime example of God's response to the adequacy issues of His servants. Born to Hebrews enslaved in Egypt, Moses miraculously escaped state-sponsored genocide. Providentially, he grew up in the palace of the very king bent on eliminating Hebrew males. An early attempt to intervene on behalf of his people against Egyptian brutality ended in a double disaster. His own people viewed him with suspicion, while he found himself on the run from the crown. In Midian, he found political refuge, a family, and a job.

Work with his father-in-law's livestock took him to Sinai.

There, the God who had called and led his ancestors arrested his life with a desert shrub that burned without burning up and with a commission more startling than the fire. God revealed that He had heard the cry of His oppressed people, and that He had come to deliver them. He would make good on promises made long ago to their ancestors. The catch? God wanted to send *Moses* to lead the task.

Between the lines, the assignment read like this: Go back to your own people, who distrust you, and to the court that has a warrant for your arrest, led by a king who thinks he's God. Organize and motivate a slave population to confront the strongest government on the face of the globe. Either overpower or elude its lavishly equipped military, and find a way out through well-guarded, national borders for the Hebrews and their things. Set up shop in the desert so these people can worship God. One more thing: tell the Canaanites you are taking their land.

Moses responded with a string of questions, beginning with "Who, me?" It was the key question of Moses' identity and personal adequacy, asked perhaps more in self-defense than for information. Then came questions of God's own identity, of Moses' credibility, and finally of his "professional" adequacy (a speech problem). Treating these defensive moves as legitimate questions, God explained and demonstrated He was fully adequate to carry out the mission He outlined. Furthermore, He would be with Moses. God would himself actually carry out the mission *through* Moses.

Finally, Moses tried to decline with the request that God send someone else. Refusal was clearly not an option. Instead, God teamed him with his brother Aaron, who would do the talking. Following a series of wonders and plagues God accomplished through Moses and Aaron, He rescued the children of Israel from Egyptian bondage. In the process, God demonstrated His saving purpose for Israel, as well as his superiority over mighty Pharaoh and the gods of Egypt (Exodus 7:17; 8:10, 22; 9:14, 16, 29). And He drew faith and celebration from His long-oppressed people (14:31—15:21).

Jeremiah: I'm Too Young!

Jeremiah lived in the roller-coaster years that saw the kingdom of Judah plunge to destruction (Jeremiah 1:1-19). In the decades just before him and on through his early years, spiritual life in Judah suffered severely. Kings Manasseh and Amon riddled Judean loyalty to God with their morally and spiritually compromised leadership (2 Kings 21; contrast 22:1—23:14). In this environment, hostile to the historic faith of Israel, the Lord told young Jeremiah of His plan that he speak as His prophet (Jeremiah 1:5, 10).

Jeremiah protested that he was just a lad, with no professional or personal clout to confront an entire nation's apostasy. As with Moses, God told Jeremiah *His* commission, *His* Word, *His* presence would make Jeremiah more than adequate and that He would rescue him from adversity sure to come.

Jeremiah came from Anathoth, home to a line of priests on the outs with the palace and the temple leadership in Jerusalem ever since the days of Solomon (1 Kings 2:26). He began to speak as the Lord's prophet when Amon's son and successor, Josiah, was just a young man (Jeremiah 1:2; 2 Kings 21:23—22:2). His prophecy supported the far-reaching reforms Josiah led when a book of the Law was found during temple renovations (2 Kings 22—23).

Jeremiah's message, however, was never popular with the crowds or leaders who resented the reforms under Josiah (Jeremiah 11:15-17). Even people from his hometown plotted to kill him (vv. 18-23). Jeremiah denounced Judah's unfaithfulness to God. Unless the people repented, he threatened, God would destroy the kingdom and their beloved temple itself at the hands of the Babylonians. When King Josiah was cut down trying to intercept Pharaoh Neco on his way north to prop up Assyria against the advancing Babylonians (about 609 B.C., 2 Kings 23:29-30), things turned ugly for Jeremiah.

Josiah's successors had no real loyalties to the Lord and tolerated criticism from no one (Jeremiah 26:20-23). The situation only worsened when the Babylonians actually invaded the land. Jeremiah claimed that they were sent by God to judge Judah, and they would destroy Jerusalem. His enemies accused him of treason. Beatings, prison, and calls for his death followed (20:1-2; 37—38). Finally, he lived under house arrest until the city fell to the Babylonians (38:28). At times, this powerful adversity led Jeremiah to despair and even tempted him to back out (15:10-11, 15-18; 20:7-18). God confronted this temptation with an invitation for Jeremiah to repent, an offer to restore Jeremiah, and a promise to carry him through the experience (15:19-21).

Jeremiah's "pro-Babylonian" stance had become known to the Babylonians. So, they took Jeremiah out of the line of captives being marched into exile and released him, with provisions to go where he wished (40:1-6). This turn of events cannot have raised his stock at all in the minds of those who had just survived the Babylonian siege. When rebels assassinated Nebuchadnezzar's governor, a contingent of Judeans fled to Egypt against Jeremiah's urging (41—43). They took Jeremiah with them but continued in Egypt the same adamant refusal to obey that had brought the judgment of God upon them in the first place. The last we hear of the prophet, he is faithfully preaching to the crowd that fled to Egypt (43—44).

So far as we know, he died in disrepute among his own people in Egypt. He had had little noticeable influence on either people or leaders during the last 25 to 30 years of his ministry. Only a very long view proved him right. Finally, the resurrection of Jesus Christ vindicated both his stern message and the new covenant vision he carried.

Gideon: I'm Too Weak!

This man's story presents puzzles from the start. He's threshing grain in a winepress, of all places, trying to hide enough food to survive another year of raids from marauding Midianites (Judges 6:1-40). Gideon wonders why the stories of God's miraculous rescues seem always to refer to times long ago or far away, and seems clueless to prophetic words that would explain his plight. The Lord's angel finds him essentially hiding in the winepress, hails him as a "mighty warrior" (v. 12), and tells him the

Lord is with him. Apparently the angel knows something about Gideon that Gideon himself does not know!

The Lord commissions Gideon on the spot to rescue Israel from these desert raiders. Gideon claims he is the nobody of nobodies: his clan is the weakest in the tribe, and he's the least significant in his family. How could he possibly rout the Midianites? God's answer? The same "I will be with you" (v. 15) speech that proved unconvincing to Gideon at the start.

God convinces Gideon he is indeed speaking to the Lord himself, prompting him to build an altar to Israel's God. Yet when the Lord's first mission strikes at the heart of this altar-building business (i.e., at the question of who really is God), Gideon's response seems garbled. It's a tough assignment. Gideon is to tear down his own father's altar to Baal and destroy an image tied to it. Family loyalties are now on the line. Gideon carries out the job, but under cover of darkness for fear of rousing opposition. He leaves his Baal-worshiping father to pose the challenge to Baal that Gideon himself should have been bold enough to make at the start.

When the story gets to the troop reduction (from over 32,000 to 300) and the rout of the Midianites for which Gideon is famous, Scripture again presents an ambiguous picture (7:1-25). He carries his Baal name into the episode—Jerub-Baal. He's still afraid. And nowhere does the Book of Judges attribute unusual courage or piety to him. By the providence of the Lord, he gets the job done, but family vengeance figures in his success (8:18-28). Finally, after sidestepping the temptation to accept royal power, he makes an instrument through which to wield priestly power (an "ephod" [v. 27]). It snares him and his people. Then at the end of the day, the Israelites failed to show kindness to Gideon's family "for all the good things he had done for them" (v. 35).

Lessons in Success—by the Book

Success is not defined by what we think of ourselves. If success began with good self-esteem, as our culture would have us think, these missions would have aborted before they began. To a man, these servants of God considered themselves inadequate for the huge venture God put to them. They correctly gauged their own utter inability to confront imperial, institutional, cultural, and family evil in their own strength. The ignorant, arrogant, and powerful people they would have to confront would indeed overwhelm them. Yet, none had taken sufficient account of God's astounding ability to make them fully adequate for whatever mission He might assign them. God's presence proved to be more than a public relations setup. It was an empowering reality. God could work through them just as they were. Success begins, not with proper *self*-esteem, but with proper *God*-esteem.

Success is not determined by what others think of us. These cases show that the opinions of others can bear significantly on our approach to obedience and our conviction of adequacy. Pressure from group feedback may even jeopardize our ability to remain faithful. Underestimating the force of these influences can sabotage any mission for God. Nevertheless, when God refocused His servants' attention away from public response and back to His own empowering presence, no opposition could dictate their future.

Public opinion turns out to be shaky ground from which to estimate our adequacy in the work of God. Other persons cannot know us as our Maker and Redeemer knows us. Many who presume to assess others' adequacy do not share priorities based on scriptural understandings of life and success. They lack the foundation to understand the "success" of persons trying to see life through the eyes of God.

Success is really defined by what God determines we can be through Him. God redefines success by rewriting the criteria for judging success. Success means hearing and obeying His Word. Success stands accountable to God's written Word and the vision He creates within us consistent with it. Success is living faithfully for Him, even and especially in the face of adversity and persecution. Because of this, success may not be recognized at all except from the vantage point of a very long hindsight.

Conclusion

Success involves not only *doing* what God sends us to do

but also *being* who God made us to be—His people, always. Thus, success entails faithfulness issues that are larger than specific tasks to which we are called. Success involves confessing—not simply as pious rhetoric but as profound awareness—that, whatever we ultimately "accomplish," God's powerful presence working through us spells the difference (the "I will be with you" factor). So success involves doing and being more than we calculate we can do on our own. Success involves living out the dream God has for us and for others through us.

About the Author: Dr. Thompson is professor of biblical studies at Asbury Theological Seminary, Wilmore, Kentucky.

THE WORLD'S VIEW

Success is making sure you are in the majority.

THE BIBLE'S VIEW

Success is standing for what is right in spite of the polls.

Joshua and Caleb

That night all the people of the community raised their voices and wept aloud. All the Israelites grumbled against Moses and Aaron, and the whole assembly said to them, "If only we had died in Egypt! Or in this desert! Why is the LORD bringing us to this land only to let us fall by the sword? Our wives and children will be taken as plunder. Wouldn't it be better for us to go back to Egypt?" And they said to each other, "We should choose a leader and go back to Egypt."

Then Moses and Aaron fell facedown in front of the whole Israelite assembly gathered there. Joshua son of Nun and Caleb son of Jephunneh, who were among those who had explored the land, tore their clothes and said to the entire Israelite assembly, "The land we passed through and explored is exceedingly good. If the LORD is pleased with us, he will lead us into that land, a land flowing with milk and honey, and will give it to us. Only do not rebel against the LORD. And do not be afraid of the people of the land, because we will swallow them up. Their protection is gone, but the LORD is with us. Do not be afraid of them."

But the whole assembly talked about stoning them. Then the glory of the LORD appeared at the Tent of Meeting to all the Israelites. The LORD said to Moses, "How long will these people treat me with contempt? How long will they refuse to believe in me, in spite of all the miraculous signs I have performed among them? I will strike them down with a plague and destroy them, but I will make you into a nation greater and stronger than they" (Numbers 14:1-12).

If serving the LORD seems undesirable to you, then choose for yourselves this day whom you will serve, whether the gods your forefathers served beyond the River, or the gods of the Amorites, in whose land you are living. But as for me and my household, we will serve the LORD" (Joshua 24:15).

4
SUCCESS AND PUBLIC OPINION

by Lonni Collins Pratt

What does it mean to be successful? If we ask a dozen people the question, we're likely to get a dozen different responses. For most of us, success is something personal, and it is associated with tangible goals: a fulfilling career; a loving marriage; well-adjusted children; owning a home, car, maybe a boat or a recreational vehicle; nice clothing; yearly vacations; and devoted friends.

In our culture we measure success in terms of what we achieve and what we own. We measure not only success in this way but God's blessing, God's approval, and whether or not we are in God's will in the same way. Christians are not exempt from embracing this definition of success, thinking that having nice things makes us impressive to others and therefore "successful."

Another Way to Think

When we delve into the history of Christianity, we find it is filled with stories of brave men and women who gave their lives for Christ. When martyrs are depicted in religious art, they often hold the instrument of their death, such as the sword that beheaded them.

With such religious art in mind, Pastor Dominic Grassi tells the story of his own near-martyrdom in his book *Bumping into God*.

He was invited to dinner by a couple he had recently married. Just hours before the expected dinner date, he had to cancel because of an emergency. He set another date with the couple for a couple weeks later and had no trouble making it for dinner that time. As they sat down to eat, he apologized again for canceling. The bride told him that it was no problem at all. She had made the lasagna about a week before their first dinner appointment. She had thawed it and just started cooking it when he called. She simply placed it back in the freezer. Then this morning, she had thawed it and cooked it again.

Pastor Grassi said that everything his Italian mother had ever told him about food spoilage came back to him "chapter and verse" as he looked at the cheese and bubbly sauce. "This lovely young girl was innocently serving me poison that looked and smelled delicious. And I had just expressed how hungry I was!"?[1]

What would be the Christian thing to do in such a situation? Suddenly suggest a craving for Chinese and offer to take them out? Feign a sudden illness? Tell the truth and embarrass the young bride who was trying so hard?

Maybe a Christian should just take a deep breath, trust God, and eat the lasagna. That's what the pastor decided to do. Later that night, he became extremely sick. He had a high fever and spent most of the night in the bathroom. Convinced he would die by daybreak, he imagined his portrait painted with one hand on his painful stomach and his other hand outstretched, holding a pan of lasagna. The title of the picture would be *Death by Lasagna*. Despite all this, he recovered by morning.

Because of the humor in this story, it is easy to overlook the struggle that went on inside this man who wanted to please the Savior he loves. For him, and for many believers, success means following God no matter what. The everyday choices we make on our spiritual journey are all about following hard after God and doing it the very best we know how.

An Unpopular Message

In Numbers 14:1-12, Joshua and Caleb delivered a message that wasn't popular to a group of people who did not want to hear it at all. They had just decided to return to Egypt. "They said to each other, 'We should choose a leader and go back to Egypt'" (v. 4). These former slaves were still thinking like people who weren't free. They were still looking behind. They were still looking for some option other than trusting God and moving forward. Joshua and Caleb told them to be strong and trust God, to stop their rebelling. The Israelites didn't like this message much, and they seriously considered stoning the two messengers.

It isn't always easy to do the right thing. It is hardly ever popular. While we can't fully understand the cultural context of the dilemma facing Joshua and Caleb, many of us know what it feels like to be the one who says the tough thing in a particular situation. Not that we're likely to have our closest friends and family threaten to stone us, but there is a price to pay, as Joshua and Caleb discovered. We can think we're doing the right thing: following God, answering to God, delivering the Word of God. Even when that is absolutely true and we're doing the best we know how, we'll be criticized. The message might be rejected—maybe even vehemently.

It could not have been easy for Joshua and Caleb to trust God either. They followed God into a possibly frightening future: a completely foreign place, an absolutely unknown place where they expected—and received—hostility. This had been a pretty harrowing experience and had required a deep, committed faith. What did they get from the people for their courage and spiritual fortitude? Rejection.

Based on the reception of their message, did Joshua and Caleb fail? Considering that no one wanted to hear them and flat out rejected what they had to say, was it a waste of their time? That's what we wonder when we face the hard questions about standing up for the right thing. About speaking out of holy convictions when there's going to be a steep price to pay. Joshua and Caleb likely stayed awake in their tents that night, wondering if it had been worth it. Were they wrong? They weren't infallible, after all. Maybe they had misunderstood God. You and I have been kept awake by those kinds of doubts too.

The Faith Factor

Rather than facing the edicts of kings to kill our children and rumors of giants in our land, you and I face obstacles to success that seem rather ordinary. We make little decisions every day about whether or not to say the courageous thing. Do we speak up and say what Christ would say in any given situation? Do we go to the people Christ would go to if He were physically with us today? To identify ourselves as Christians means to identify with the mission and work of Christ. That will put us in contact with the struggling ones—the weak, the poor, the homeless, and the spiritually blind.

"I can do everything through him who gives me strength" (Philippians 4:13) was Paul's calm declaration of faith. No matter what, we are able to do the right thing—even the hard and unpopular thing—because our faith enables strength, the strength that only God gives.

Equipped for Swimming Against the Tide

Whether or not others agree is irrelevant when it comes to doing the right thing. Something isn't right simply because a majority of people believe it. At the same time, something isn't necessarily right because a minority of people believe it. Right or wrong, truth or error is always determined in relation to God.

As Christians, our primary source for determining if something is right or wrong is the Bible. It is a witness to the Word of God among us and contains important criteria for determining if something is right or wrong. There are some clear-cut answers in the Bible. Murder is always wrong. Adultery is still a sin. We have an obligation to the weaker ones and to the poor. Jesus is the only hope of the universe. God is the Creator of all that is.

However, we cannot always open the Bible to "chapter and verse" answers when a question arises. Our fast-changing society often creates dilemmas in which we must use all our Christian experience, tradition, and reasoning ability to determine the right thing to do.

What should we do when the question is whether to eat or

not to eat the lasagna? Should we call something false when others see only its glittering facade? What do we do when we find out a coworker is having an affair? What do we do when a teacher is being unfair to our children? What about when a church leader acts out of selfish ambition rather than concern for the community he or she is called to nurture? A boss lies, a spouse cheats, a friend make a decision that we're sure is heading him or her for disaster. What's a Christian to do?

There are no simple answers. Yet, if the Scriptures have been transplanted into our spirits, we will find the courage to behave as God wants us to act. The Word of God is alive in believers who pray, study, and live it. For them it becomes second nature. The substance of the Scripture becomes the substance of their lives.

Such Christians have learned to follow the advice found in S. D. Gordon's *Quiet Talks on Prayer.*

> Read prayerfully. We learn how to pray by reading prayerfully. This Book [the Bible] does not reveal its sweets and strength to the keen mind merely, but to the Spirit enlightened mind. All the mental keenness possible, with the bright light of the Spirit's illumination, . . . is the "open sesame." . . . Fight shallowness. Insist on reading thoughtfully. A very suggestive word in the Bible for this is "meditate." Read obediently. As the truth appeals to your conscience, let it change your habit and life.[2]

Prayer, like reading the Bible, is not something we turn to only during a crisis. There are answers, comfort, and strength in Holy Scripture and in prayer as it is mined in its depths over time. As it becomes a beloved habit, it accomplishes the work of re-creating us. It is not merely a formula to be followed only when we need a resolution to a problem.

When we face a difficult decision or situation, when we want very much to do the right thing, we should pray. But we should also make prayer and Scripture a daily part of our lives. If we don't pray, if we don't study, we may lose the desire, or even the ability, to pray. As we train ourselves to pray and read every day without fail, we grow in our awareness of God's presence. Then God speaks to us simply and quietly in those confusing moments when the right thing to do is not clear. And He gives us the courage to take a stand for something bigger than ourselves, no matter how unpopular the truth may be.

When we hear the challenge, as we do in so many ways in our anti-Christian culture, "choose . . . this day whom you will serve," we can respond like Joshua. "As for me and my household, we will serve the Lord" (Joshua 24:15).

Notes

1. Dominic Grassi, *Bumping into God* (Chicago: Loyola Press, 1999), 111-14.

2. S. D. Gordon, *Quiet Talks on Prayer* (New York: Grosset and Dunlap, 1940), 186.

About the Author: Lonni Collins Pratt is a Christian freelance writer from Lapeer, Michigan.

THE WORLD'S VIEW

"Look out for No. 1."

THE BIBLE'S VIEW

Redefines who No. 1 is.

Ruth

In the days when the judges ruled, there was a famine in the land, and a man from Bethlehem in Judah, together with his wife and two sons, went to live for a while in the country of Moab. The man's name was Elimelech, his wife's name Naomi, and the names of his two sons were Mahlon and Kilion. They were Ephrathites from Bethlehem, Judah. And they went to Moab and lived there.

Now Elimelech, Naomi's husband, died, and she was left with her two sons. They married Moabite women, one named Orpah and the other Ruth. After they had lived there about ten years, both Mahlon and Kilion also died, and Naomi was left without her two sons and her husband.

When she heard in Moab that the LORD had come to the aid of his people by providing food for them, Naomi and her daughters-in-law prepared to return home from there. With her two daughters-in-law she left the place where she had been living and set out on the road that would take them back to the land of Judah.

Then Naomi said to her two daughters-in-law, "Go back, each of you, to your mother's home. May the LORD show kindness to you, as you have shown to your dead and to me. May the LORD grant that each of you will find rest in the home of another husband."

Then she kissed them and they wept aloud and said to her, "We will go back with you to your people."

But Naomi said, "Return home, my daughters. Why would you come with me? Am I going to have any more sons, who could become your husbands? Return home, my daughters; I am too old to have another husband. Even if I thought there was still hope for me—even if I had a husband tonight and then gave birth to sons—would you wait until they grew up? Would you remain unmarried for them? No, my daughters. It is more bitter for me than for you, because the LORD's hand has gone out against me!"

At this they wept again. Then Orpah kissed her mother-in-law good-by, but Ruth clung to her.

"Look," said Naomi, "your sister-in-law is going back to her people and her gods. Go back with her."

But Ruth replied, "Don't urge me to leave you or to turn back from you. Where you go I will go, and where you stay I will stay. Your people will be my people and your God my God. Where you die I will die, and there I will be buried. May the LORD deal with me, be it ever so severely, if anything but death separates you and me." When Naomi realized that Ruth was determined to go with her, she stopped urging her (Ruth 1:1-18).

Esther

The king was sitting on his royal throne in the hall, facing the entrance. When he saw Queen Esther standing in the court, he was pleased with her and held out to her the gold scepter that was in his hand. So Esther approached and touched the tip of the scepter.

Then the king asked, "What is it, Queen Esther? What is your request? Even up to half the kingdom, it will be given you."

"If it pleases the king," replied Esther, "let the king, together with Haman, come today to a banquet I have prepared for him."

"Bring Haman at once," the king said, "so that we may do what Esther asks."

So the king and Haman went to the banquet Esther had prepared. As they were drinking wine, the king again asked Esther, "Now what is your petition? It will be given you. And what is your request? Even up to half the kingdom, it will be granted."

Esther replied, "My petition and my request is this: If the king regards me with favor and if it pleases the king to grant my petition and fulfill my request, let the king and Haman come tomorrow to the banquet I will prepare for them. Then I will answer the king's question" (Esther 5:1-8).

So the king and Haman went to dine with Queen Esther, and as they were drinking wine on that second day, the king again asked, "Queen Esther, what is your petition? It will be given you. What is your request? Even up to half the kingdom, it will be granted."

Then Queen Esther answered, "If I have found favor with you, O king, and if it pleases your majesty, grant me my life—this is my petition. And spare my people—this is my request. For I and my people have been sold for destruction and slaughter and annihilation. If we had merely been sold as male and female slaves, I would have kept quiet, because no such distress would justify disturbing the king."

King Xerxes asked Queen Esther, "Who is he? Where is the man who has dared to do such a thing?"

Esther said, "The adversary and enemy is this vile Haman" (Esther 7:1-6).

5
SUCCESS AND SELF-INTEREST

by Melanie Starks Kierstead

Ruth and Esther were bold women of great faith. Each was an alien in a foreign land, without protection of husband or father. They teach us that faith in God sometimes calls us to step out and do for others even though it may be at great personal cost. These women ignored their own self-interests to care for God's people. They rejected the socially prescribed roles behind which they could have hidden in the name of self-preservation. They became *selfless* to care for the ones they loved.

Ruth's Shameful Heritage

The story of Ruth is more than a story of women bonding. It is a story of God rewarding sacrifice with great honor. Although Ruth would become the great grandmother of King David and, consequently, an ancestor of our Lord, remarkably, she would not have been considered a member of the chosen race. In fact, if we trace her heritage, she was a Moabite, a shamed race descended from Moab who was the son of Lot's incestuous relationship with his daughter.

Ruth's is a love story of loss, faithfulness, and reward. Living along the fertile southeastern edge of the Promised Land, Ruth married a famine refugee from Bethlehem, who soon died, leaving her childless and destitute. In the days of close-knit clans, Ruth had taken on the shame of marrying a man not only outside her clan but also a foreigner in her country of Moab.

She suffered the shame of widowhood when he died, and

she remained committed to her also-widowed mother-in-law, Naomi. Although she was under no obligation to stay with Naomi, Ruth recognized that Naomi was also in need of protection. What little bit she might offer, she made available to her mother-in-law. She and her sister-in-law, Orpah, lived with their mother-in-law until Naomi announced that this foreign land had left her raw with grief, and if she must die destitute, she preferred to do so in her homeland. Naomi was prepared to return to Bethlehem in Judah alone.

When Naomi announced that she was leaving Moab to return to Judah, she encouraged her daughters-in-law to do the socially honorable thing and return to their own families, who would care for them, protect them, and perhaps find other husbands for them. Naomi, on the other hand, was an old, foreign widow with no means of support, having lost her husband and sons in the country of Moab. Naomi's daughter-in-law Orpah followed her sage advice and returned to her family, who would see that she was remarried and had children to grow up and protect her.

Ruth Honors Naomi

Ruth, on the other hand, made a powerful statement of commitment to Naomi, Naomi's people, Naomi's land, and Naomi's God. There were no return trip plans for her. She intended to stay and see that Naomi was cared for in her old age, regardless of the certainty of her own ongoing widowhood. It is impossible to think that she could have considered a trip to Judah and living there an easier life than returning to her own family.

For the good of Naomi, she accompanied her to Bethlehem, where they presented themselves as widows to Naomi's kinfolk. As was common, the kinfolk did what little they needed to do so as to not bring shame upon the members of their family. For the honor of Naomi's family, Ruth was allowed to go along behind the grain harvesters and collect what was left over so that she and her mother-in-law would not starve. For the honor to be found in a new husband, God's choice, Boaz, was in place. He fell in love with Ruth when he witnessed her faithful devotion to

Naomi's well-being. He put aside her foreignness, her shameful heritage, and embraced the beauty of her character. When Ruth shouldered the responsibility of making Naomi her mother, God honored her abandonment of self-interest by himself becoming her own personal Father-Protector.

Esther and Her People

In many ways, Esther's story is much like Ruth's. Esther was a foreigner, a lowly member of the exiled Jewish people living under Persian rule. She herself was an orphan, raised by a kinsman, Mordecai. One might even suggest that it is Mordecai who is the hero of the story. However, assuming that it is Esther who is the protagonist, this is a perfect plot for a story that depicts that it is God, not people of nobility, who has the greater influence. Like the courageous shepherd boy who God used to overcome the giant and later ascend the throne, the hero of the Esther story is most unlikely, except that we know that God enabled her to make the right choices.

Choices Becoming for a Queen

Esther was presented with a series of choices. She *chose* to honor her benefactor Mordecai when he requested her to go through the candidate-for-queen preparations. A reasonable question would be: What girl could resist the possibility of becoming a queen? Considering the outcome of her predecessor, it seems that Esther reasonably could refuse. In many ways, her path would be difficult, perhaps dangerous, and certainly unsure. She would live outside her social circles and set herself up for the possible humiliation of rejection by the pagan king.

However, if she were selected, she would be queen to an egomaniac king who had deposed the previous freethinking queen, Vashti. Nevertheless, following the insights of her guardian, Esther *chose* to prepare herself for review. For months, Esther was pampered, primped, and finally paraded before Xerxes who did select her to be his queen. This made for more choices. Once Esther became queen, she could have easily segregated herself from her relative and the masses of Jews. Yet, we know that she *chose* to maintain her clandestine relationship with Mordecai, her mentor and coach.

A Queen Committed to Duty

Upon hearing, by way of Mordecai, of Haman's evil plot to exterminate the Jews, at first Esther was beside herself. She had no idea what to do. She called the Jewish people to fast and pray —to seek God's wisdom as to what could be done. She *chose* to remain true to her understanding that God was God, even over the pagans, especially when she learned of Haman's scheme to have the Jews destroyed. It becomes clear to us that when she fasted and prayed, she understood that God alone would determine her people's destiny. We could say, when she called her people to pray, she became something of a religious leader, a prophet, if you will, in the days of no prophecy. What she was to do is revealed to us only after we see the value she placed in seeking God's favor.

Much is made of Esther's uninvited appearance before Xerxes, but she had already demonstrated courage. Self-interest had been displaced by godly courage and understanding of what she had been called to do. With grace and dignity that God inspired, Esther went directly to the king's court. Interestingly, this queen did not do as some might do. She did not employ bedroom politics, ingratiating herself with sexuality to be heard by the king. And her call on the king was clearly not a social call. Instead, by entering the court of the king, she established that she had come, indeed, to do business. He recognized her and seemed to be fascinated as much by her courage as he had been by her beauty.

However, in a strange twist of events, she turned the business call into an invitation to Xerxes and Haman to come to a feast. As much as her bravery, it was her cunning that is praised when she fed the stomach of her enemy at the table of her king. The plot thickens as Xerxes' curiosity was aroused at the feast and was met with yet a second invitation. By then, his curiosity was thoroughly piqued. Haman was so sated that he was blindsided by her revelation and accusation that he was trying to kill her and her people. The dinner party came to an abrupt end! Emotions were running high all around the table. The king, outraged and humiliated by Haman's bigoted ineptitude, sent him out to be killed—to be replaced by none other than Mordecai.

Repeatedly, Esther *chose obedience over self-interest* as God put her in the place where He could use her. Her appointment as queen, Mordecai insisted, was a divine appointment for God's service. Her beauty and grace, which enchanted King Xerxes, paralleled the beauty of her character, which allowed her to be employed by the King of the universe.

Children of the King

These women, attuned and intolerant to injustice, surrendered what they had, great and small, because they were determined to see that good was done. They are in great company throughout history. Common and not so common women like Deborah—a judge of Israel—Joan of Arc, Catherine of Siena, Hannah Whithall Smith, Catherine Booth, and Mother Teresa all model for us what it is to trust God to give direction on how to combat injustice.

Who should be next to abandon self-interest and risk losing position, reputation, or life that injustice may not go forward? Who will step out and raise the battle cry for children of this century who are, in one way or another, to one degree or another, put out to die? Who will speak for children who, while playing, trip a buried land mine? Who will speak for the children who live on dumps and celebrate another day of being alive? What lone voice will cry out for children trained for guerrilla warfare before they reach puberty? Who will bravely stand up against the "make the best of it" tide and say a child needs a caring and loving family? What voice will risk criticism and misunderstanding to begin a dialogue about responsible roles of the media and sports stars? Who will it be who insists that their children will grow up respectful of authority and all humanity? Who will call for racial reconciliation? Who will it be who rallies hope for suicidal teenagers who see no way around purposeless existence? Who will protect and comfort the elderly and infirm? Who will fast, pray, and remain unswerving in commitment to overturning laws that allow abortion for convenience? Better yet, who will be wise enough to *seek God's ways* to expose acts of injustice? Who will be courageous enough, abandoning self-interest, to capture attention of those who have no idea that an entire nation at their door is about to perish?

Like Ruth, who demonstrated disregard for her own personal well-being because of her faith in Naomi's God, believers are assured that it is no sacrifice to give up what one cannot keep to have that which cannot be taken away. Like Esther, who sought God's wisdom to protect His people, stated with dignity and conviction, "If I perish, I perish" (4:16). Their stories, without the hesitation of self-interest, demonstrate that God honors courageous, obedient faith by becoming the Defender of the defenseless and the Father of the fatherless.

About the Author: Dr. Kierstead is professor of biblical literature at Asbury College and an ordained minister in The Wesleyan Church.

THE WORLD'S VIEW

I am entitled to success and the good life.

THE BIBLE'S VIEW

All that we have is a gift from God.

Job

In the land of Uz there lived a man whose name was Job. This man was blameless and upright; he feared God and shunned evil. He had seven sons and three daughters, and he owned seven thousand sheep, three thousand camels, five hundred yoke of oxen and five hundred donkeys, and had a large number of servants. He was the greatest man among all the people of the East.

His sons used to take turns holding feasts in their homes, and they would invite their three sisters to eat and drink with them. When a period of feasting had run its course, Job would send and have them purified. Early in the morning he would sacrifice a burnt offering for each of them, thinking, "Perhaps my children have sinned and cursed God in their hearts." This was Job's regular custom.

One day the angels came to present themselves before the LORD, and Satan also came with them. The LORD said to Satan, "Where have you come from?"

Satan answered the LORD, "From roaming through the earth and going back and forth in it."

Then the LORD said to Satan, "Have you considered my servant Job? There is no one on earth like him; he is blameless and upright, a man who fears God and shuns evil."

"Does Job fear God for nothing?" Satan replied. "Have you not put a hedge around him and his household and everything he has? You have blessed the work of his hands, so that his flocks and herds are spread throughout the land. But stretch out your hand and strike everything he has, and he will surely curse you to your face."

The LORD said to Satan, "Very well, then, everything he has is in your hands, but on the man himself do not lay a finger."

Then Satan went out from the presence of the LORD.

One day when Job's sons and daughters were feasting and drinking wine at the oldest brother's house, a messenger came to Job and said, "The oxen were plowing and the donkeys were grazing nearby, and the Sabeans attacked and carried them off. They put the servants to the sword, and I am the only one who has escaped to tell you!"

While he was still speaking, another messenger came and said, "The fire of God fell from the sky and burned up the sheep and the servants, and I am the only one who has escaped to tell you!"

While he was still speaking, another messenger came and said, "The Chaldeans formed three raiding parties and swept down on your camels and carried them off. They put the servants to the sword, and I am the only one who has escaped to tell you!"

While he was still speaking, yet another messenger came and said, "Your sons and daughters were feasting and drinking wine at the oldest brother's house, when suddenly a mighty wind swept in from the desert and struck the four corners of the house. It collapsed on them and they are dead, and I am the only one who has escaped to tell you!"

At this, Job got up and tore his robe and shaved his head. Then he fell to the ground in worship and said:

"Naked I came from my mother's womb,
and naked I will depart.
The LORD gave and the LORD has taken away;
may the name of the LORD be praised."

In all this, Job did not sin by charging God with wrongdoing (Job 1:1-22).

6

SUCCESS, I DESERVE IT!

by Richard K. Eckley

Job was a righteous man. That was never in question. Everyone who lived around his neighborhood in Uz spoke well of him. From their various social vantage points, they watched him prosper and rise to power. They witnessed the babies being added to his household. They envied the parties thrown at his luxurious estate. Even when the economy was going south, the growth of Job's empire was always heading up. At some time or another, each of them had said, "I wish I had what Job has. I wish I were blessed like Job."

Being blessed was all Job had ever known. He had come from a good family that had taught him the value of faithfulness to God. He had done all the right things, made all the right choices. In the end, God's promises to reward those who obeyed Him had paid off. Actually, if the truth were told, it took a lot of hard work—mixed with this religious devotion—but Job did believe, and he was quick to tell others of that belief. God was good to Job, and Job knew it.

Yet, one day all of that changed. Again the neighbors watched. They watched as Job's life fell apart. The odds of this happening to any one man were astronomical. First, the Sabeans came and took his oxen. Then, fire from heaven consumed his sheep. The Chaldeans stole his camels. All of his servants were killed in the process. It was as if the powers of the universe had turned on him. When the tornado came through the town, everyone knew that he had been cursed. The great wind avoided all of the buildings and people in the area, touching down only on Job's family. By day's end, his whole family was dead, with the exception of his wife.

That was a sad day. Job and his wife were not in the building when it collapsed, but all that Job truly loved had been destroyed in that disaster. His culture and values were motivated by the perpetual gift of life in a person's children. People around town, who had been a bit jealous of his expanding families, were now just a little relieved, even secretly joyful to see Job struggle with his family. What kind of people would be glad that such calamity would befall another person? The woman down the street, for one, who had been barren all her life, who had to face the jeers of the mothers in the public square, was glad. The family, whose two children had left to follow faraway morals and lifestyles, were glad to see another family fall apart, no matter how it had to happen. On that day, all of the hardworking folks in the country, those whose sweat had never reaped success, realized that Job was just like them. And they were glad.

Yet, even on that day, Job worshiped his God and was heard to say, "The LORD gave and the LORD has taken away" (1:21). He understood the value of his family, and he would have gladly died that they might live. Still, he was thankful for the short time of blessing. He would not turn his back on God.

Then the sores came, with the painful suffering and the personal humiliation. He had hit the lowest point in his life. The blessings were all gone. Being righteous was no longer fun.

Like any man would, Job became reflective. Job, the successful businessman, was reduced to a philosopher on an ash heap. The "why" question was at the end of his blistered tongue. His wife and his friends added their suggestions to his own search for self-analysis. "Why has this happened to me?" Job cried out, in effect. "I have done everything I was asked! I deserve a little success in my life!" He may have remembered all of his past conversations about the poor. From his successful perch, he was able to hand out advice on how to reap the same benefits. If they would only work harder. If they would just put their faith in God. If they would only do what he did. The rich have always had a plan for the poor. Now others had plans, advice, and suggestions to give Job. All he could do was sit there and listen.

Sound Economic Advice

When Job was perched on the pinnacle of his success, few would have come by to offer any suggestions on how he might invest, develop, or extend his capital. Now they came out of the woodwork. Like callers to a radio talk show, they all knew exactly what needed to be done. They all had an economic plan that always worked. They understood the causes of poverty and how easily it could be fixed.

Some came to say success is based on cause and effect. If you work hard, you get success. Conventional wisdom had always believed this. The roots of this proverbial wisdom came from believing in a good God. This good God had placed into the design of creation a certainty that if you work with the system, the system will work with you. This philosophical logic worked well. All the clichés in the world were derived from it in some way: "A penny saved is a penny earned." "God helps those who help themselves." "The early bird gets the worm." And the list goes on.

The cause-and-effect system worked the other way as well, so they thought. Since disaster had come upon Job, something sinful and lacking in Job must be the cause. Faced with the reality of human infirmity, Jesus' disciples would later ask Him in relation to a blind man: "Who sinned, this man or his parents, that he was born blind?" (John 9:2). Though it has always been popular to blame someone else for our failures and weaknesses, Jesus did not enter into that speculation. He merely picked up at the point of a person's life and brought healing.

Some came to pronounce the inevitable: Job may as well "curse God and die" (2:9). Offending God was not to be taken lightly. Job may as well take the consequences and be done with it.

Job's Self-Justification

One after another, Job's well-meaning neighbors—even the wife that he loved—left with the same verdict: your lack of success proves that God is no longer on your side. Yet, Job knew he had not broken the rules. He trusted God with his life.

Other men had gone through similar problems. Bankruptcy at the end of a risky business venture. Cancer after years of smoking and disdain for good health. We have seen our share of ruined households, mostly, it was thought, because of the shaky foundations of humanistic, worldly values. Yet, now Job was one of the statistics, and he didn't like it. All of these other cases of failure appeared to be so easy to decipher, but his case was different—at least from his perspective.

In the end, Job understood that there was no easy answer, no formula for success. His friends' advice only added to his suffering. He sent them away with these words:

> Everything you say, I have heard before. I understand it all; I know as much as you do . . . But my dispute is with God, not you. . . . You cover up your ignorance with lies; you are like doctors who can't heal anyone. Say nothing, and someone may think you are wise! (13:1, 3-5, TEV).

If ever there was a man who had learned the lesson of Jesus' words to "not worry about tomorrow, for tomorrow will worry about itself" (Matthew 6:34), it was Job. Even before knowing about the possibilities of life through the resurrection of our Lord, Job was reflecting on the future. He had learned to do first things first and put the blessings that would follow second. Even if he were never to find the success he had once tasted, he would have known God, and that was worth all of this suffering.

Still, that did not stop him from being angry. "Patience" is not the best way to describe Job's attitude; "perseverance" is better. He was done with such "good advice," and he expected God to vindicate him. He let his voice be heard. He was frustrated and angry—and he let God know it.

God's Final Word

Well, finally God showed up—in a whirlwind. Though it would appear that Job had justified his own righteousness, God was not impressed with even that argument. God's ways are indeed unique. To Job's self-justification, even self-pity, God recounted His creative powers of the inanimate universe, then went on to the animal kingdom. Finally, God merely pointed to His own place as Creator and decried any need to support His actions. Debates over whether Satan was at the root of these calamities or whether God ordained and directed such suffering are not even discussed. God is God. And that is that. In the end, God does not have to reward anyone's faithfulness. As He asked Job, "Who has a claim against me that I must pay? Everything under heaven belongs to me" (41:11).

In all his attempts to figure out why, he still remained faithful to God. This is the only thing that makes sense in the midst of suffering. God told Job's friends that their advice was wrong, and that Job had spoken what is right. Job was right because he closed his mouth and listened to God. God does reward this kind of faithfulness—in His time and in His way.

The last chapter of Job completes the story of his successful life like a bookend. The very question that Job pondered—if you do good, don't you deserve success?—is finally answered. After this ordeal of both body and spirit, God returned Job's blessings in multiples. Finally, a simple answer to the complex question: Why do bad things happen to good people? The answer: Good people do finally get it all in the end.

But is the answer that simple? What if the story had ended without this final reckoning—as it has for so many other people on this earth? Job got back his health, his livestock, and his houses. He may even have found his quiver full again with laughing, playing children. Would this ever replace the family he had lost? Could such material blessing ever be the balm that cools the searing pain of his memories? Even this happy ending begs for a sequel. The Final Judgment alone will provide a complete reward for all good and faithful servants.

In the end, success is not reduced to even these material things. The question posed by Satan (the Adversary) that spurred this story on in the first place was now answered. "Does Job fear God for nothing?" (1:9). Yes! True success had been found in experiencing the God who blesses, not the blessings themselves. Job was a better man for having gone through his sufferings than if he had never done so. He had come to meet God. A holy God had proved him righteous, and that is success enough.

Our attitudes toward success are so imbedded in us that we often can't separate the biblical values from those of our culture. Middle-class social values placate our sense of God's grace and support. When we receive promotions and paychecks, we often have the sense that our hard work has paid off, that our bootstraps have been stretched just a bit more in our pulling them up. Somehow we walk away with the idea that we deserve what we get—both success for ourselves and failure for others.

The Judeo-Christian values of work and success are related to blessing, but only in that God chooses whom He wishes to bless, impartially to the just and unjust. We are asked to participate in the great occupation of life with a steadfast resolve to do what is best for the whole. In the end, God may choose to rain down His blessings upon us, or we may have to find such joy in the future. To question God is to reveal our lack of understanding of God's place and person.

Many people today wish to separate the world into categories of the rich and the poor, the blessed and the cursed. Moral judgments are often related to this caste system. In this system, the poor and the rich somehow deserve their social status. We learn from Job's life that such "cause and effect" remains a part of the mystery of life. Christians are pleased to work hard and to contribute to the common good, but the blessings of our work are always something for which we are thankful. Sometimes our hard work does not have much immediate reward.

The father of the modern sociology of religion, Max Weber, showed that the basis of the American capitalist system was the so-called Protestant work ethic. Religious and social forces mixed together to form the fuel for the rapid growth in American economic history. Farmers in the early agricultural system, and later the factory workers in the Industrial Revolution, both understood that hard work would be rewarded with success and prosperity. Generally, this is true. Still, most of us do not live in the luxury of generalities. Many people who work hard never see material gain. Just as many people who never worked a day in their lives end up with "the lives of the rich and famous." Like Job, we today have a lesson to learn that there is no automatic connection between hard work and success—except when God becomes the causal link himself.

In studies of the history of human thought, quite often the Book of Job is included in anthologies right along with the writings of Plato, Aquinas, and Hegel. The questions concerning human destiny and due are never probed more beautifully than in the suffering of this ancient man, Job. Christians still have much to learn in the deep reflections of someone who came to see God in the midst of his problems. Our modern culture is still attempting to understand the nature of true success as it relates to the extremes of life. Job stands the test of time as a witness that ultimate success is found in discovering the mystery of God's providence and grace.

About the Author: Dr. Eckley is associate professor of theology at Houghton College, Houghton, New York. He is an ordained minister in The Wesleyan Church.

THE WORLD'S VIEW

We have everything we need to be successful. We can pull ourselves up by our own bootstraps.

THE BIBLE'S VIEW

God is the Source of all things. Success has to do with a proper vision of who God is.

Isaiah

In the year that King Uzziah died, I saw the Lord seated on a throne, high and exalted, and the train of his robe filled the temple. Above him were seraphs, each with six wings: With two wings they covered their faces, with two they covered their feet, and with two they were flying. And they were calling to one another:

"Holy, holy, holy is the LORD Almighty;
the whole earth is full of his glory."

At the sound of their voices the doorposts and thresholds shook and the temple was filled with smoke.

"Woe to me!" I cried. "I am ruined! For I am a man of unclean lips, and I live among a people of unclean lips, and my eyes have seen the King, the LORD Almighty."

Then one of the seraphs flew to me with a live coal in his hand, which he had taken with tongs from the altar. With it he touched my mouth and said, "See, this has touched your lips; your guilt is taken away and your sin atoned for."

Then I heard the voice of the Lord saying, "Whom shall I send? And who will go for us?"

And I said, "Here am I. Send me!"

He said, "Go and tell this people:

"'Be ever hearing, but never understanding;
be ever seeing, but never perceiving.'
Make the heart of this people calloused;
make their ears dull
and close their eyes.
Otherwise they might see with their eyes,
hear with their ears,
understand with their hearts,
and turn and be healed."

Then I said, "For how long, O Lord?" (Isaiah 6:1-11).

7
THE SOURCE OF SUCCESS

by John N. Oswalt

What produces success?

There are two views. One says that our success is entirely a product of our own effort and ambition. The other says that while our effort and ambition are important, they are not the essential ingredients. In fact, success achieved by those means alone will always evaporate.

An article in a recent *Smithsonian* magazine tells of a reporter who was, in the early years of the 20th century, among the best-known people of the day. He made himself famous by his coverage of the Spanish-American war in Cuba and of the Boer War in South Africa. Yet, when he died suddenly in 1916, all his fame disappeared overnight. Today he is virtually unknown. No effort, ambition, or even talent are enough to secure real success.

So what is the necessary ingredient for lasting success? It is found in the story of Isaiah. Although we do not know for certain, all the indications are that Isaiah was marked early for success. He seems to have been a member of the royal family with all of the good breeding and educational opportunities such a birth implies. Yet, he tells us that in the end those things were of little account. He had an experience that changed his whole perspective on this issue and helped him realize what really mattered.

The Whole Earth Is Filled with His Glory

In 739 B.C., Uzziah, king of Judah, died. It was like a great oak tree had suddenly fallen. While Uzziah was alive, it was possible to ignore what was happening to the north. Now the sky was no longer obscured by that tree's abundant foliage. Now the boiling black clouds of a thunderstorm hurtling toward them were plain to see. That storm was the mighty Assyrian empire pushing southward toward its eventual conquest of Egypt. Although Jotham, Uzziah's son, had been coregent with his father, he was not the person to stem that storm. What were they to do?

This is what was burdening the mind of the young Isaiah as he trudged up the hill to the Temple that day. What could Judah do? What could *he* do? What was his responsibility? Could he do something to save his nation from the terrible fate that seemed to be rushing down upon it? Would he succeed if he dedicated his considerable talent in a terrific effort of will?

Whatever Isaiah expected when he went to the Temple that day, we can confidently say it was not what actually happened to him. What happened was totally unexpected. It was an overwhelming moment that changed him forever. That breathtaking glimpse of the holiness of God, His absolute *otherness*, stayed with him all his life. We know it did because of Isaiah's favorite title for God, "the Holy One of Israel (Jacob)." This title occurs 31 times in the Bible, and 27 of them are from Isaiah's pen.

What happened in this event to create genuine success in Isaiah's life? We can identify six components: a vision of God, a vision of himself, the receiving of God's provision, the awareness of God's desire, the offering of himself, and the willingness to submit his own definition of success to God's definition.

A Vision of God

Along with God's absolute holiness, His perfection in every regard, Isaiah also got a glimpse of the true source of glory. The seraphim cried out, "The whole earth is full of his glory" (Isaiah 6:3). What does that mean? In the Old Testament "glory" is not something thin and passing, as it has come to mean in modern times. Instead, it is the very opposite. It is weightiness and significance. It is solid and enduring. This is true glory, isn't it? True glory is what we human beings really want. We want to do something that will endure after we have left this earth. We want people to notice us and think we are important.

That is what the ancient people were doing when they built the temple towers all over southern Mesopotamia. The greatest of these is told about in Genesis 11 in the incident we know as "The Tower of Babel." They were trying to capture the power of God "to make a name for" themselves (v. 4). They thought that if they built this great tower, they could bring God down to earth and make His power subservient to them. Surely all future generations would say, "What a glorious thing those people did! What a success they made of themselves! What glory they gained!" In fact, according to the Bible, that attempt to glorify themselves only brought confusion to the earth.

Isaiah learned better. He saw that any glory he achieved apart from total submission to God was going to be hopelessly contaminated. The only real weight and significance in this world belongs to the Creator of this world. He is the only being in existence who can truly say, "I AM" (Exodus 3:14). He exists in himself and is not dependent on any other thing for His existence. He alone has glory. Everything else in the universe derives its existence from Him. And any attempt by any created thing to glorify itself apart from Him must inevitably fail.

Vision of Himself

We can imagine that as Isaiah heard the glorious voices of the seraphim praising God, the only Holy One, that he thought, "Oh, I wish I could do that. I wish I could tell the world who God really is in words like that. Wouldn't people be impressed?" Yet, with the piercing clarity that a vision of God gives, Isaiah knew it would never happen. Even the most gorgeous words in the world coming out of his lips would be hopelessly corrupted and contaminated. Isaiah knew that any attempt to achieve glory for himself would not only fail but also corrupt whatever it touched.

Why is that? What was it Isaiah had seen? In the light of God's purity, Isaiah had glimpsed a fundamental fact of human existence—the putrefying power of human self-will. One aspect of God's holiness is that everything He does is turned outward in sacrificial love. This is the relationship that the Persons of the Trinity enjoy with each other, and this is the Trinity's relationship with all of creation. That is not the case with humans. From the hour when our first parents concluded they had to supply their needs for themselves (as if they could!), we, their children, have been cursed with this contaminating desire to draw everything in toward ourselves. The outcome is described vividly in Genesis 6:5: "Every inclination of the thoughts of [the human] heart was only evil all the time." The sense of the verse in Hebrew is that the very way we go about shaping the images in our minds is corrupt. That is because everything we want, we want in order to consume it ourselves.

What's the answer then? Can we ever succeed? Can we ever participate in, or share, that genuine glory, the glory of the Creator? Isaiah's answer is an unqualified yes! We certainly can, if we will do three things—three things that really boil down to one. That one thing is the next thing that happens in the story, and it makes possible the following two. It is an experience of purification. Something has to happen that will purify our will, that will turn it outward, away from ourselves and toward others. For Isaiah, that something was an experience of fire, fire that burns up the trash and purifies the steel.

A seraph came to him with a coal off the altar in a pair of tongs. If it was too hot for a seraph (in Hebrew, a "burning one") to hold in his hand, it was truly hot! Would Isaiah submit to that? Suppose he felt his greatest talent was his ability to speak. Would he submit to having that gift perhaps consumed, perhaps taken from him forever? Would he submit to the pain of having whatever was trash in himself exposed and consumed? Fortunately, he did submit. Why? Because he understood that to retain his gift for himself would ultimately destroy both him and those he tried to use it on. He would be like a surgeon who refuses to give up a rusty butcher knife with which he expects to do surgery. Isaiah understood that there is no other road to true success than to allow God to do whatever He wishes with his talents and abilities.

Receiving God's Provision

Surely it is no accident that the next thing that happens in the story is that Isaiah hears the voice of God for the first time in this account. We do not know if God had been speaking before this or not. Nevertheless, if He had, Isaiah was in no condition to hear Him. Isaiah had been full of his own plans, his own desires, his own fears. Now that Isaiah had lost everything to God and in so doing had gained everything, now that his own glory was not the ruling principle in his life, he was able to hear the voice of God. Notice that, while Isaiah 6 is often referred to as "the call of Isaiah," there is no commanding call here. It is almost as if the Trinity was quietly communing among themselves and Isaiah was eavesdropping: "Whom shall I send? And who will go for us?" (v. 8). To surrender our glory for God's glory is to begin to become sensitive to the heart of God. Now that our success and importance no longer fill our minds, we begin to hear the quiet, but insistent beating of the heart of God. So Isaiah, full of wonder that he is alive and not blasted to a cinder, full of joy that his gift is no longer filthy but clean, leaps up crying, "Oh, could you use me?" Here is no reluctant victim forced into some divine scheme. Here is one astounded that the Holy One might have a place for him.

Awareness of God's Desire

Yet, there is one more part of this success story, one that is often eliminated when we retell this story. It is easy to see why it would be eliminated. It is not pleasant at all. When God tells Isaiah what his message is to be, it is not what we want to hear. We want God to tell Isaiah to go declare a message of divine love that will turn the whole nation back to God. We want God to tell Isaiah that he is to be the messenger of a great revival. But that is not what God says. He tells Isaiah he is to speak a word that will blind the eyes, deafen the ears, and harden the hearts of his hearers. To this, the newly cleansed Isaiah does not say, "What?" or "Why me?" He only says, "How long?" (v. 11). God's shocking answer is that Isaiah must speak this message until the whole nation is like a field of burned-over stumps. What's going on here?

Offering of Himself

While the answer to the question is not explicit, it seems to be rather clear in the context. Isaiah could have preached a watered-down message that might have met with a good deal of apparent success. Maybe there would have been a superficial turning to God, a superficial healing, which could have been very gratifying to Isaiah. Yet if that had happened, there would have had to be another prophet of the Messiah. It would not have been Isaiah. Isaiah would have been just one more of the false prophets, helping the people to paper over their sins without really addressing them.

In fact, God knew that if Isaiah were really faithful, if he really declared the full truth of the situation, Isaiah's generation would not repent. Instead, they would simply be hardened in their determination to have their own way. These people have now gone so far that the only possible cure for the nation is through the fires of judgment. A superficial cure would only delay the inevitable and might indeed obscure the truly desperate nature of the situation. On the other hand, if Isaiah will faithfully declare the truth and be willing to bear the apparent failure of his preaching, then there will be a lamp lighted that will shine through the darkness. It will be there, not only for the handful of his own day who will hear it and faithfully preserve it, but also for a future generation on the other side of the fire, a generation that will hear the full message and truly repent. Then there will spring up from one of those burned-out stumps, the stump of Jesse, a new green shoot, the Messiah of God (11:1).

Willingness to Submit

Thus, the final point of this story is that real success is defined in terms of faithfulness to God, and not in terms of what this world calls success. With hearts that have been cleansed and turned outward, we, like Isaiah, can gladly accept God's definition and not our own. In the end, that is the true meaning of success.

About the Author: Dr. Oswalt is research professor of Old Testament at Wesley Biblical Seminary in Jackson, Mississippi. He is the author of five books and is a noted Isaiah scholar.

THE WORLD'S VIEW

Religion and wealth are separate issues in life.

THE BIBLE'S VIEW

To serve Christ, we must give everything over to God.

The Rich Young Ruler

A certain ruler asked him, "Good teacher, what must I do to inherit eternal life?"

"Why do you call me good?" Jesus answered. "No one is good—except God alone. You know the commandments: 'Do not commit adultery, do not murder, do not steal, do not give false testimony, honor your father and mother.'"

"All these I have kept since I was a boy," he said.

When Jesus heard this, he said to him, "You still lack one thing. Sell everything you have and give to the poor, and you will have treasure in heaven. Then come, follow me."

When he heard this, he became very sad, because he was a man of great wealth. Jesus looked at him and said, "How hard it is for the rich to enter the kingdom of God! Indeed, it is easier for a camel to go through the eye of a needle than for a rich man to enter the kingdom of God."

Those who heard this asked, "Who then can be saved?"

Jesus replied, "What is impossible with men is possible with God."

Peter said to him, "We have left all we had to follow you!"

"I tell you the truth," Jesus said to them, "no one who has left home or wife or brothers or parents or children for the sake of the kingdom of God will fail to receive many times as much in this age and, in the age to come, eternal life" (Luke 18:18-30).

Paul

Finally, my brothers, rejoice in the Lord! It is no trouble for me to write the same things to you again, and it is a safeguard for you. . . .

If anyone else thinks he has reasons to put confidence in the flesh, I have more: circumcised on the eighth day, of the people of Israel, of the tribe of Benjamin, a Hebrew of Hebrews; in regard to the law, a Pharisee; as for zeal, persecuting the church; as for legalistic righteousness, faultless.

But whatever was to my profit I now consider loss for the sake of Christ. What is more, I consider everything a loss compared to the surpassing greatness of knowing Christ Jesus my Lord, for whose sake I have lost all things. I consider them rubbish, that I may gain Christ and be found in him, not having a righteousness of my own that comes from the law, but that which is through faith in Christ—the righteousness that comes from God and is by faith. I want to know Christ and the power of his resurrection and the fellowship of sharing in his sufferings, becoming like him in his death, and so, somehow, to attain to the resurrection from the dead (Philippians 3:1, 4-11).

8
THE PRICE OF SUCCESS

by Carl M. Leth

He was the kind of young man that you hope your daughter will bring home. He was the kind of young adult that you are anxious to have in your church. You would be pleased to have him on your church board. He was everything you would hope to find in a church leader. He was gracious, financially prosperous, and scrupulously attentive to the demands of his religious faith. So, what's the problem?

That's the question that troubled the rich young ruler (see Luke 18:18-30). The problem was that there seemed to be something missing. He was still looking for something. Despite his obvious success, something prompted him to seek Jesus out. "All that I have," he seems to say, "has not given me what I am seeking." He hoped that Jesus could help him find it.

Perhaps he was looking for Jesus' approval, for Jesus to say, "You're OK," or "You're a great guy." Or, maybe there was some overlooked portion of the Law that was the key. It could be that he thought Jesus had some secret teaching or wisdom that would complete his success. It may be that he didn't have any idea what the secret was, only a sense of his need. What he had achieved wasn't enough. He was looking for something from Jesus.

A Walking Success Story

It was difficult for the audience that watched this encounter with Jesus—and for us—to imagine what could be missing. He had all the "right stuff." The story begins as a virtual catalog of the young man's success. Courteous, even flattering, he calls Jesus "good teacher" (v. 18). To address Jesus in this way was a gracious expression of respect. His manner reflects personal grace.

To his gracious manner he added personal wealth. He was a person of unusual means and personal prosperity. He surely reflected the benefits of education and personal refinements that often accompany wealth. That would be impressive enough, but there was more. To his culture, his wealth implied not only personal success but also divine approval. It was understood to be a sign of God's blessing. "God likes you," he thought his wealth declared.

On top of all that, he was a faithful congregation member. He followed the rules. His moral life was exemplary. He paid his tithe. He did all the right things. What a guy! He embodied success. He was the fulfillment of what many of us hope to be.

The Response He Didn't Expect

Amazingly, Jesus disagrees. His response stunned the rich young ruler and the crowd around Him—including His disciples. "Nice try," Jesus seems to say, "but you've missed the mark. What you need to do is to take your wealth, which is a demonstration of your success and God's approval, and give it away. Take your life, which is so full of signs of your personal and religious success, and give it away and follow Me alone. If you want to be successful, you must abandon your success."

Is it any wonder that the rich young man was perplexed and distressed? What Jesus had said hardly even made sense. Who wouldn't be confused?

A Different Kind of Success Story

Perhaps we can more clearly understand the story of the rich young ruler by looking at another success story. In Philippians 3:3-11 Paul explains how he redefined success in his life. He, too, had all the "right stuff," he tells us. His credentials were impeccable. He had the right degrees and connections. He was a fellow on the fast track. He had achieved success.

Then Paul discovered that his success was really failure in disguise. His old measures for successful performance paled by comparison with a different kind of success. What he owned or what he had accomplished were no longer the benchmarks for achievement of success. Paul had found a new measure. It redefined what true success was.

Paul's standard for success was no longer what he could achieve, but who he could become. His success would no longer be found in what he could do or produce, but in who he was.

A New Measure for Success

Paul discovered a new measure for the success of his life. It was, simply, Christ. Success now meant to be transformed into His likeness, to be like Him, to share His life—and His death. To succeed was to order all of life by this one purpose, this one goal—to be a person transformed by Christ.

The price of such a radical form of success was the surrender of all other forms of success. All of Paul's other claims to achievement and significance are set aside. They are, by comparison, nothing. They no longer factor into the assessment of the success of Paul's life. They don't count any more. All other standards of success fall short of this one goal, to be a person transformed into the likeness of Christ.

The rich young ruler had to surrender his wealth as the justification of his claim of success. He had to surrender his life as the demonstration of his success. He heard Jesus' uncompromising demand to abandon all other means to success for the sake of this one alone. He faced the same demand that Paul confronted, but he came to a different conclusion. He decided that the price was too high.

Answering the Difficult Question

We don't know what happened to the young ruler. He went away saddened that he had failed to find the object of his search at a price he was willing to pay. What he failed to see was the high cost of his decision. While we don't know the details of his later life, we can confidently project its likely course. It is a lifescript that has often been replayed on the stage of history.

In our own time, Howard Hughes serves as an emphatic example. As a young man he was handsome, wealthy, and socially gracious. His strong intellectual and creative gifts added to a can't-miss profile for success. He had all the "right stuff." He assembled a list of impressive accomplishments. He should have been a model for success, but he ended his life in isolation and madness. The focus of his life circled around his own self-interest in an ever-narrowing spiral until he consumed himself. The person who seemed to be a sure prospect for success epitomized personal failure.

We live in a time of successful achievers. We live in a society that idolizes, almost worships, images of success. We are motivated to accomplish. We are driven to acquire. We only know how to trade up to a bigger house, a better job, a more expensive car, a more prominent position. Success has become a virtual obsession.

The story of the rich young ruler is almost 2,000 years old, but it is as timely as this morning's paper. Like that young man, we come dragging our successes behind us, looking for something. Our bag of successes is never quite full enough. It never quite satisfies. There is still something missing.

The reason is that our passionate search for success has taken us in the wrong direction. We're asking the wrong question. We keep asking, "What must I *do*?" All the possible answers to that question leave us short of the answer for the really important question. The key question for true success is, "Who should I *be*?" Success is not about what I have. It's not really about what I have achieved. Success is, finally, about who I am. Jesus' answer to that question is that who we are should be defined by following Him.

Like Paul, we are called to abandon all other standards for this single measure of success. Our success is no longer determined by what we have done, but by who we follow.

Knowing a Rich Young Ruler When You See One

It is easy to read the story of the rich young ruler when we assume that its message is for someone else. Those of us who are not wealthy or especially successful can relax as we observe "their" discomfort in the face of this rigorous challenge. We can sympathize with them as they face Christ's absolute demand to surrender their most precious treasures, but we are spectators observing the struggle of the rich to make it through the "eye of a needle" (Matthew 19:24; also Mark 10:25 and Luke 18:25). Certainly the story highlights the difficulty of the rich to accept Christ's demands. Still, it doesn't end there.

Jesus' response to the rich young ruler echoes the call that He gives to each of us. He demands the surrender of all of our "stuff." Some of the "stuff" that He wants us to surrender looks pretty spiritual. Maybe we're like the rich young ruler after all. That is, maybe we're not rich, but we keep all the rules, we say the right things, we do the right actions. We can testify to the right religious experiences. We are religious success stories. Jesus says, "Surrender that success to Me."

Perhaps it is not only the financially wealthy who have trouble fitting through the eye of the needle. Perhaps those of us who carry a wealth of hard-won spiritual success have a difficult time too. As impressive as that success might be, it falls short of the measure Paul describes—to rest our success in Christ alone.

This is the word I hear Christ speak to me. It is a difficult word, troubling to hear. I want to bring all the evidence of my religious and spiritual achievements. I want to stand out from the crowd of ordinary Christians, my banners of accomplishment declaring my success. Christ calls me to put them aside and follow Him, content to glory only in Christ.

Successful Poverty

God's economy of success works in baffling ways. The rich young ruler walked away a failure—despite his position, wealth, and religious achievements. Paul discovered success by abandoning his achievements, credentials, and religious status. Or perhaps we should express that in a different way. Paul didn't reject all of those things, he simply reprioritized his value system. Once his standard for success was to follow Christ—to know Him, and to be like Him—all those other measures of success were, by comparison, worthless.

If you ask Paul—and, I think, Jesus—whether you are successful, he will not ask your pedigree or the size of your bank account. He will not ask whether you won the Sunday School attendance award or how long you have served on the church board. He won't even ask if you can give the right testimony about your religious experiences. He will simply ask if Christ is so much the central focus of your life that you are being transformed into His image and character. Nothing else is even worth talking about.

About the Author: Dr. Leth holds a Ph.D. from Duke University in church history. He is pastor of Detroit First Church of the Nazarene.

THE WORLD'S VIEW

The position, power, money, and influence we have in the world are human measures of success.

THE BIBLE'S VIEW

God does not measure success by human standards.

The Widow

As he looked up, Jesus saw the rich putting their gifts into the temple treasury. He also saw a poor widow put in two very small copper coins. "I tell you the truth," he said, "this poor widow has put in more than all the others. All these people gave their gifts out of their wealth; but she out of her poverty put in all she had to live on" (Luke 21:1-4).

Mary

In the sixth month, God sent the angel Gabriel to Nazareth, a town in Galilee, to a virgin pledged to be married to a man named Joseph, a descendant of David. The virgin's name was Mary. The angel went to her and said, "Greetings, you who are highly favored! The Lord is with you."

Mary was greatly troubled at his words and wondered what kind of greeting this might be. But the angel said to her, "Do not be afraid, Mary, you have found favor with God. You will be with child and give birth to a son, and you are to give him the name Jesus. He will be great and will be called the Son of the Most High. The Lord God will give him the throne of his father David, and he will reign over the house of Jacob forever; his kingdom will never end."

"How will this be," Mary asked the angel, "since I am a virgin?"

The angel answered, "The Holy Spirit will come upon you, and the power of the Most High will overshadow you. So the holy one to be born will be called the Son of God. Even Elizabeth your relative is going to have a child in her old age, and she who was said to be barren is in her sixth month. For nothing is impossible with God."

"I am the Lord's servant," Mary answered. "May it be to me as you have said." Then the angel left her (Luke 1:26-38).

9
THE MEASURE OF SUCCESS

by Stephen Lennox

If success is defined as what someone would die for, most would measure it by money, power, and influence. God provides a different definition of success in the opening verses of Luke 21. In this passage, Jesus teaches that true success has almost nothing to do with what we have or who we are.

Though brief, this story is long on insight into God's view of success. The hero is a poor widow, a member of what may have been the most vulnerable, most abused, and most helpless group in Jesus' day. Yet, because of her sacrifice, Christ held up this widow as a model of success.

Teachers of the Law

Jesus was sitting in one of the courtyards in the Temple. "Opposite" him (Mark 12:41), in full view, were the 13 receptacles that received contributions from the people. Each box was shaped like a trumpet, with the wider part at the bottom and the narrow opening at the top.[1] On each box was an inscription, identifying the purpose for its contents. The contributions placed in one box were used to buy wood for burning the sacrifices. Those in another were used to buy the incense burned on the altar. There was a box to contribute to the upkeep of the golden vessels and so forth. Jesus watched intently as people approached, chose their box, and deposited their offering.

The mention of a "poor widow" at the beginning of Luke 21 draws a definite connection between this episode and Jesus' harsh words at the end of chapter 20. The two stories contrast the humble, generous widow with the self-righteous, honor-seeking teachers of the law, who grew rich at the expense of women like this.

Teachers of the law (scribes) were highly respected members of that society. Well-educated by ancient standards, they were considered experts in the Law of Moses. A Jewish book written around the time described in the gospel provides insight into how Jesus' contemporaries viewed the scribe. In it we learn that a scribe

> concentrates his mind and his meditation on the Law of the Most High. He researches into the wisdom of all the Ancients, he occupies his time with the prophecies. He preserves the discourses of famous men, he is at home with the niceties of parables. He researches into the hidden sense of proverbs, he ponders the obscurities of parables. He enters the service of princes, he is seen in the presence of rulers. He travels in foreign countries, he has experienced human good and human evil.

Not only was the scribe well-educated and well-traveled, but this Jewish book also points out his piety.

> At dawn and with all his heart he turns to the Lord his Creator; he pleads in the presence of the Most High, he opens his mouth in prayer and makes entreaty for his sins. If such be the will of the great Lord, he will be filled with the spirit of intelligence, he will shower forth words of wisdom, and in prayer give thanks to the Lord. He will grow upright in purpose and learning, he will ponder the Lord's hidden mysteries. He will display the instruction he has received, taking his pride in the Law of the Lord's covenant.

According to this same source, scribes were highly respected among the people.

> Many will praise his intelligence and it will never be forgotten. His memory will not disappear, generation after generation his name will live. Nations will proclaim his wisdom, the assembly will celebrate his praises. If he lives long,

his name will be more glorious than a thousand others, and if he dies, that will satisfy him just as well.[2]

When Jesus criticized "the teachers of the law" (Luke 20:46) he attacked men who were highly honored as righteous and wise. Many of these men, however, had strayed far from God's ideal of wisdom and piety. Although there were some who still sought righteousness (see Mark 12:28-34), Jesus blasted the warped standards of success so prized among them. Their flowing robes identified them as wealthy men with elevated social status. Their clothing also signified leisure, since flowing robes are useless to those who must work for a living. Perhaps Jesus mentioned the robes first to highlight the misplaced priorities of those who wore them. They loved being recognized in the marketplace. To sit in the best seats in the synagogues and banquet halls filled them with pride. One scholar says the people considered the scribe worthy of more respect than one's own parents.[3]

The scribes relished this respect, not from pride alone, but because of the power it brought. Wherever they went, their opinion mattered most, and other people had to seek their favor. These men used this power to their advantage in numerous ways. Frequently invited to dinner, they fed their appetites from others' tables. Even worse, they gobbled up the homes of poor widows.

Perhaps they impoverished poor women by demanding support for their "teaching ministry." They may have cheated them in unscrupulous business dealings. Some commentators suggest that older husbands chose a scribe, a man with a sterling reputation for piety, to serve as trustee for their estate on behalf of the husband's wife and children. Perhaps Jesus criticized those scribes who abused their trustee role by cheating widows of their rightful inheritance.

Defining "success" by money, honor, and power is bad enough; it is worse when the "successful" are really hypocrites. We dislike unscrupulous businesspersons who take advantage of others without regard for what we or God think of them. Even worse is the cheat who tries to hide corruption behind a veneer of religion. Such were many of the scribes. They prayed "lengthy prayers" (Luke 20:47) so they could trap more victims. It would be easy to think, "Who would make a better trustee to provide for a widow than a man who publicly prays long prayers?"

Their prayers fooled some people, but not God. Although applauded by their fellow Jews as popular, wealthy, and powerful—in a word, successful—Jesus says that God will punish the scribes "most severely" (v. 47). What a contrast to the widow in 21:2. Everything the scribes had, she lacked. Yet, Jesus publicly applauded her and publicly condemned them.

A Teachable Moment

Luke used a very unusual word found only here in the New Testament—"lepta," which means "thin one."[4] The widow dropped two copper coins (lepta) into the offering box. These two coins, which together were not even worth one modern penny, constituted "all she had to live on" (v. 4). Some commentators suggest that givers had to announce their contribution amounts when dropping their gifts into the boxes. If this is true, this practice would have further humiliated the widow and other poor worshipers.

Jesus turned the scene into a teachable moment on the definition of true success. He must have shocked His listeners when He announced, "This poor widow has put in more than all the others" (v. 3). To emphasize His point, Jesus began with, "I tell you the truth" and then referred to the woman in a way that emphasized her poverty (literally in Greek, "the widow, the poor one"). To His bewildered listeners, Jesus explained that all the others, particularly the "rich" of 21:1, gave out of their abundance, while the widow gave out of her extreme poverty. She gave not only a very large amount compared to what she possessed but all she had to live on.

Clearly, Jesus did not measure generosity by the amount given but by the amount that remained. Success, according to Jesus, has less to do with what we have than with what we have left over after we have given to God. Even more remarkable is that Jesus commended her for sacrificing for the Temple, a building that would shortly be reduced to rubble (the theme of the following passage, Luke 21:5-6). Her gift went to buy supplies for a sacrificial system that Jesus' death and resurrection, within one week, would render obsolete. Her sacrifice was not only miniscule but wasted. Still, even a wasted sacrifice, when given sacrificially to God, is a mark of great success.

Redefining Success

This widow's action must cause us to redefine success. Those who appeared successful—the scribes with their power, influence, and wealth—were actually failures marked for punishment. Nor would they be spared because they prayed or gave to the Temple. This woman, with none of the trappings of success, received a hearty well-done from God, in spite of the fact that her gift was essentially wasted.

God does not base success on the amount we sacrifice. He who multiplied the contents of one box lunch to feed thousands is not impressed by our gifts (see John 6:1-13). Success in His eyes begins in a willing, humble spirit that gives not grudgingly or for prestige, but because "the giver cannot help it."[5] This is what Paul says in 2 Corinthians 8:12. Addressing this church on the matter of giving to others, he reminded them that "if the willingness is there, the gift is acceptable according to what one has, not according to what he does not have." Count on it, giving like this inevitably means sacrifice. Wiser heads would have told her to hold back something for a rainy day. Yet, she could not help it; she had to give. Hers was a reckless sacrifice.

This attitude of sacrificial and humble obedience can be found at the core of a truly successful person. One thinks of Mary, the mother of Jesus. As a teenaged maiden, she was anything but successful in the eyes of the world. Yet, when called to a lifetime of faithful and painful obedience to God, she responded, "I am the Lord's servant. May it be to me as you have said" (Luke 1:38).

As Jesus criticized the "successful" scribes and pronounced their doom, so Mary's song celebrated the same reversal.

My soul glorifies the Lord and my spirit rejoices in God my Savior, for he has been mindful of the humble state of his servant. From now on all generations will call me blessed, for the Mighty One has done great things for me— holy is his name. . . . He has brought down rulers from their thrones but has lifted up the humble. He has filled the hungry with good things but has sent the rich away empty *(Luke 1:46-49, 52-53).*

Christians must not be fooled into evaluating success—their own or someone else's—by the wrong standards. Wealth, power, influence, or honor cannot determine true success. Nor can true success be determined by what we accomplish, even what we accomplish in God's name. When we sacrificially and humbly obey God, then we have succeeded.

Notes

1. William Barclay, *The Gospel of Luke,* in *The Daily Study Bible Series* (Philadelphia: Westminster Press, 1975), 254.

2. Patrick W. Sehan and Alexander A. DiLella, *Wisdom of Ben Sira,* in *Anchor Bible Series* (New York: Doubleday, 1987), 39:1-11.

3. Barclay, 253.

4. Ibid., 255.

5. Ibid.

About the Author: Dr. Lennox is chairperson of the religion and philosophy division at Indiana Wesleyan University. He is the author of commentaries on Psalms and Proverbs, published by Wesley Press.

There are no second chances after failure.

We believe in the God of second chances.

Judas

While he was still speaking, Judas, one of the Twelve, arrived. With him was a large crowd armed with swords and clubs, sent from the chief priests and the elders of the people. Now the betrayer had arranged a signal with them: "The one I kiss is the man; arrest him." Going at once to Jesus, Judas said, "Greetings, Rabbi!" and kissed him (Matthew 26:47-49).

Early in the morning, all the chief priests and the elders of the people came to the decision to put Jesus to death. They bound him, led him away and handed him over to Pilate, the governor.

When Judas, who had betrayed him, saw that Jesus was condemned, he was seized with remorse and returned the thirty silver coins to the chief priests and the elders. "I have sinned," he said, "for I have betrayed innocent blood."

"What is that to us?" they replied. "That's your responsibility."

So Judas threw the money into the temple and left. Then he went away and hanged himself (Matthew 27:1-5).

Peter

Now Peter was sitting out in the courtyard, and a servant girl came to him. "You also were with Jesus of Galilee," she said.

But he denied it before them all. "I don't know what you're talking about," he said.

Then he went out to the gateway, where another girl saw him and said to the people there, "This fellow was with Jesus of Nazareth."

He denied it again, with an oath: "I don't know the man!"

After a little while, those standing there went up to Peter and said, "Surely you are one of them, for your accent gives you away."

Then he began to call down curses on himself and he swore to them, "I don't know the man!"

Immediately a rooster crowed. Then Peter remembered the word Jesus had spoken: "Before the rooster crows, you will disown me three times." And he went outside and wept bitterly (Matthew 26:69-75).

Afterward Jesus appeared again to his disciples, by the Sea of Tiberias. It happened this way: Simon Peter, Thomas (called Didymus), Nathanael from Cana in Galilee, the sons of Zebedee, and two other disciples were together. "I'm going out to fish," Simon Peter told them, and they said, "We'll go with you." So they went out and got into the boat, but that night they caught nothing.

Early in the morning, Jesus stood on the shore, but the disciples did not realize that it was Jesus.

He called out to them, "Friends, haven't you any fish?"

"No," they answered.

He said, "Throw your net on the right side of the boat and you will find some." When they did, they were unable to haul the net in because of the large number of fish.

Then the disciple whom Jesus loved said to Peter, "It is the Lord!" As soon as Simon Peter heard him say, "It is the Lord," he wrapped his outer garment around him (for he had taken it off) and jumped into the water. The other disciples followed in the boat, towing the net full of fish, for they were not far from shore, about a hundred yards. When they landed, they saw a fire of burning coals there with fish on it, and some bread.

Jesus said to them, "Bring some of the fish you have just caught."

Simon Peter climbed aboard and dragged the net ashore. It was full of large fish, 153, but even with so many the net was not torn. Jesus said to them, "Come and have breakfast." None of the disciples dared ask him, "Who are you?" They knew it was the Lord. Jesus came, took the bread and gave it to them, and did the same with the fish. This was now the third time Jesus appeared to his disciples after he was raised from the dead.

When they had finished eating, Jesus said to Simon Peter, "Simon son of John, do you truly love me more than these?"

"Yes, Lord," he said, "you know that I love you."

Jesus said, "Feed my lambs."

Again Jesus said, "Simon son of John, do you truly love me?"

He answered, "Yes, Lord, you know that I love you."

Jesus said, "Take care of my sheep."

The third time he said to him, "Simon son of John, do you love me?"

Peter was hurt because Jesus asked him the third time, "Do you love me?" He said, "Lord, you know all things; you know that I love you."

Jesus said, "Feed my sheep" (John 21:1-17).

10
SUCCESS AND FAILURE

by Gaymon Bennett

Like Simon Peter, Judas Iscariot was chosen by Jesus Christ to be His disciple. For three years he walked, talked, ate, and ministered with Jesus and the other disciples. He was an eyewitness to the miracles of Jesus and seemed sensitive to his earthly mission. Like Peter, Judas failed Jesus in His hour of greatest need. However, Judas was destroyed by his failure, while Peter sought forgiveness, and God transformed his failure into success.

Judas

Relatively little is known about Judas. He is mentioned among the first 12 disciples and, according to the Gospel of John, was the treasurer of the group. Like the others, he heard the parables of the lost sheep with its image of the seeking shepherd and the lost son with its drama of forgiveness. He would have been near when Jesus healed the lepers, the lame, and the blind. He would have been in the boat when Jesus calmed the storm and among those who gathered the leftovers when Jesus fed the hungry crowd.

In Bethany when Mary poured expensive perfume over Jesus' feet, Judas asked, "Why wasn't this perfume sold and the money given to the poor?" (John 12:5). John, in his account of the scene, impugns Judas's motives, but the statement implies that Judas understood Jesus' compassion for the poor.

Yet Jesus knew that Judas planned to betray Him, though the other disciples were shocked by the revelation. When, at the

Last Supper, Jesus said, "One of you will betray me" (Matthew 26:21), they reacted with sad surprise.

One after another they said, "Surely not I, Lord?" (v. 22).

Jesus answered cryptically, "The one who has dipped his hand into the bowl with me will betray me" (v. 23).

Even Judas protested, "Surely not I, Rabbi?" (v. 25), even though he had already struck a deal with the high priests to hand Jesus over to them for "blood money" of 30 silver coins.

The Betrayal

The story of the actual betrayal is familiar. Jesus, accompanied by the other disciples, had gone to Gethsemane to pray. Jesus instructed His companions to watch and pray while He walked a little way from them into the darkness, fell to the ground, and pleaded, "Father, if it is possible, may this cup be taken from me. Yet not as I will, but as you will" (v. 39). When Jesus returned, He found the disciples sleeping and chided them for not watching with Him. Twice more He went away from them to agonize and twice returned to find them sleeping.

Suddenly they were jolted awake by torchlight and noise as a large, armed mob, led by Judas, confronted them. By pre-arrangement, Judas identified Jesus to the crowd by greeting Him. Seized and arrested, Jesus went willingly with His captors but reproached them. "Am I leading a rebellion, that you have come out with swords and clubs to capture me? Every day I sat in the temple courts teaching, and you did not arrest me. But this has all taken place that the writings of the prophets might be fulfilled" (vv. 55-56).

We can only conjecture about Judas' motivation. Perhaps he assumed that Jesus would escape miraculously. Perhaps he thought he would be forcing the issue of Jesus' messiahship. We cannot know exactly what John's description means: "Satan entered into him" (John 13:27). However, it is clear that when he realized that Jesus would be condemned and executed, Judas suffered remorse. We can suppose he thought that, by giving back the money, he could right the wrong he had done. Yet, when he tried to return the 30 silver coins with the words, "I have sinned, . . . for I have betrayed innocent blood," the chief priests replied unfeelingly, "What is that to us? . . . That's your responsibility" (Matthew 27:4).

Judas reacted by throwing the coins into the Temple and rushing out to hang himself. Was he overwhelmed by the enormity of his sin? Did the burden of his responsibility for betraying his Friend, his Teacher, his Lord seem too great to bear? Did he conclude from Jesus' words at supper, "Woe to that man who betrays the Son of Man" (26:24), that he was beyond forgiveness? Whatever the reasons for his actions, Judas's choice foreclosed the possibility of redemption and restoration.

Peter

In contrast to our lack of information about Judas, we know a lot about Simon Peter. He is the first-mentioned of the disciples in Matthew's Gospel. He and his brother Andrew were mending their fishing nets when Jesus called them, and they threw down the nets and readily followed Jesus. Peter was the first to confess that Jesus was "the Christ [or Messiah], the Son of the living God" (16:16). Jesus blessed him for his insight and declared that He would build the Church on Peter's confession.

Six days after that confession, Jesus took Peter, James, and John to a mountaintop. There Jesus, in the presence of Moses and Elijah, was transfigured, His face shining like the sun and His clothes gleaming white as light. Peter enthusiastically declared that it was good for the disciples to have experienced the event and offered to erect shelters to honor all three. As Peter spoke, the presence of God enveloped them like a cloud, and God said, "This is my Son, whom I love; with him I am well pleased" (17:5).

The Denial

Still, it wasn't many months after this stunning revelation that Jesus predicted Peter's infamous denial. Just hours before the disciples' ordeal in Gethsemane, Jesus told them that they would desert Him.

Peter said, "Even if all fall away on account of you, I never will" (26:33).

To which Jesus replied, "This very night, before the rooster crows, you will disown me three times" (v. 34).

Peter wouldn't let it drop and declared, "Even if I have to die for you, I will never disown you" (v. 35). It seems like an impulsive reaction, and Peter is often caricatured as rash and full of bluster, but it's the answer most Christians would give. And, in fact, all the other disciples instantly echoed Peter's declaration.

That night in Gethsemane, as Jesus was being led away to face the high priest Caiaphas and the Sanhedrin, all the disciples did desert Him. All, with the temporary exception of Peter, ran away. Peter hung around outside in the courtyard. Perhaps he thought he could maintain a safe distance or hide in the darkness. However, while he skulked there, a servant girl approached him.

"'You also were with Jesus of Galilee,' she said" (v. 69).

His response was to deny it to everyone around. Then he added, "I don't know what you're talking about" (v. 70).

We can imagine his embarrassment and shame as he tried to slip away. Yet, he made it only as far as the gateway before another girl—just a girl, not a threatening or armed guard—pointed him out to the crowd. "This fellow was with Jesus of Nazareth" (v. 71).

Peter denied it again, this time with an oath. "I don't know the man!" (v. 72) he shouted.

Perhaps more to resolve the matter than to accuse him, some of the people in the crowd reasoned with Peter. "Surely you are one of them, for your accent gives you away" (v. 73).

Exasperated and angry, Peter called down curses upon himself, and he swore, "I don't know the man!" (v. 74). Immediately the rooster crowed, Peter recalled the words of Jesus, and he ran out into the night, weeping bitterly.

The Restoration

Matthew says nothing more about Peter specifically after that episode. John, however, picks up the story when Peter encountered Jesus by the Sea of Galilee, where he had returned to his fishing. Peter and six of his friends and fellow disciples had fished all night with no luck, when in the early morning light they saw a man on shore hailing them.

The man, whom they didn't recognize yet, shouted, "Friends, haven't you any fish?" (John 21:5). When they answered that they hadn't, He called back, "Throw your net on the right side of the boat and you will find some" (v. 6).

Of course, when the disciples did as He suggested, they netted so many fish they almost couldn't haul them in. At this point, John, putting two and two together, realized that the man on shore was Jesus.

He said to Peter, "It is the Lord!" (v. 7). As soon as Peter heard it, he jumped out of the boat and splashed ashore, swimming and running to Jesus.

There Jesus had made a fire of coals over which He was grilling breakfast. He called to them to bring some of the fish they had just caught, and Peter eagerly climbed back aboard the boat and dragged the net ashore.

After breakfast, in a bittersweet scene, Jesus asked Peter, "Do you truly love me more than these?"

"Yes, Lord," Peter replied, "you know that I love you."

Jesus responded, "Feed my lambs" (v. 15).

Jesus asked twice more if Peter loved Him, and the third time Peter—distraught and hurt—said, "Lord, you know all things; you know that I love you."

And Jesus repeated, "Feed my sheep" (21:17).

The implication is clear: Jesus had restored Peter to his calling as disciple. It seems worth pointing out that when Judas failed, he ran from Jesus, while Peter ran to Him, seeking restoration, professing his love, and implying his willingness to follow and serve his Lord. After Pentecost, Peter was successful despite his earlier failures.

The Optimism of Grace

It may be difficult for most of us to identify with Judas. We can't imagine betraying Jesus with malice aforethought, yet, in our human frailties, we are certainly capable of betrayal. It is surely easier for us to identify with Peter. We can imagine—and most of us can recall—making impulsive promises that we could not keep, rash declarations of faith that we were unable to fulfill. Nevertheless, God's grace is available for betrayal as well as failure, for the core of God's character, revealed throughout Scripture, is forgiveness. When Moses interceded for his rebellious people, the "gracious God, slow to anger, abounding in love and faithfulness" (Exodus 34:6) forgave them. When David asked God to forgive him for treachery and adultery, God cleansed him and restored the joy of his salvation. God's grace is not merely available but, according to the apostle Paul, is "abundant" (Romans 5:17).

Judas's action in this story clearly demonstrates what happens when we do not choose to seek forgiveness. Peter, in contrast, represents the possibility of restoration, which is the message of hope in the face of failure. Such restoration doesn't come about because of our human efforts. Even Spirit-imparted knowledge is no guarantee against human failure. When Peter recognized that Jesus was the Messiah, Jesus said, "This was not revealed to you by man, but by my Father in heaven" (Matthew 16:17). Peter also saw Jesus transfigured and proclaimed, "Lord, it is good for us to be here" (17:4). Yet, equipped with such powerful knowledge, he still deserted Jesus in Gethsemane, disowned Him outside the court, and didn't show up for His crucifixion.

The Bible promises forgiveness and restoration, if we confess our sins. Jesus' seeking out Peter at the seaside implies His eagerness to forgive. His telling Peter, in Matthew 18:22, that he should forgive his brother, not 7 times but 77, suggests the limitlessness of God's forgiveness, for He would not ask us to do what He would not do for us. Indeed, our spiritual "success" may be measured by both our being forgiven and our forgiving as God in Christ forgave us.

The Bible also promises that in our being justified before Christ we become new creations; we are given a brand-new start. I can remember my preacher-father defining the term "justify" as just-as-if-I had never sinned. We can then, like Peter, be not only forgiven but transformed—made new.

One hot August afternoon when our oldest daughter was about three, we rode bikes to a nearby drive-in to buy ice-cream cones. Before long, Cristina's ice cream had begun to melt and drip down the cone and onto her little fist. She held the drippy mess up to me and said, "Make it new, Daddy." I licked the contours of the cone clean, wiped her hand with a napkin, and gave the cone back, much to her satisfaction.

How wonderful it is to know that God will do even better: blot out our past failures, give us success, and make us new—all for the asking.

About the Author: Dr. Bennett teaches American literature, writing, and secondary language arts education at Northwest Nazarene University, Nampa, Idaho.

THE WORLD'S VIEW

All the right moves lead to climbing the "ladder of success."

THE BIBLE'S VIEW

The only right moves are the ones that keep God at the center of our lives.

Daniel

But Daniel resolved not to defile himself with the royal food and wine, and he asked the chief official for permission not to defile himself this way. . . .

Daniel then said to the guard whom the chief official had appointed over Daniel, Hananiah, Mishael and Azariah, "Please test your servants for ten days: Give us nothing but vegetables to eat and water to drink. Then compare our appearance with that of the young men who eat the royal food, and treat your servants in accordance with what you see." So he agreed to this and tested them for ten days.

At the end of the ten days they looked healthier and better nourished than any of the young men who ate the royal food (Daniel 1:8, 11-15).

Then Daniel went to Arioch, whom the king had appointed to execute the wise men of Babylon, and said to him, "Do not execute the wise men of Babylon. Take me to the king, and I will interpret his dream for him." . . .

"The great God has shown the king what will take place in the future. The dream is true and the interpretation is trustworthy."

Then King Nebuchadnezzar fell prostrate before Daniel and paid him honor and ordered that an offering and incense be presented to him. The king said to Daniel, "Surely your God is the God of gods and the Lord of kings and a revealer of mysteries, for you were able to reveal this mystery" (Daniel 2:24, 45-47).

So the king gave the order, and they brought Daniel and threw him into the lions' den. The king said to Daniel, "May your God, whom you serve continually, rescue you!"

A stone was brought and placed over the mouth of the den, and the king sealed it with his own signet ring and with the rings of his nobles, so that Daniel's situation might not be changed. Then the king returned to his palace and spent the night without eating and without any entertainment being brought to him. And he could not sleep.

At the first light of dawn, the king got up and hurried to the lions' den. When he came near the den, he called to Daniel in an anguished voice, "Daniel, servant of the living God, has your God, whom you serve continually, been able to rescue you from the lions?"

Daniel answered, "O king, live forever! My God sent his angel, and he shut the mouths of the lions. They have not hurt me, because I was found innocent in his sight. Nor have I ever done any wrong before you, O king."

The king was overjoyed and gave orders to lift Daniel out of the den. And when Daniel was lifted from the den, no wound was found on him, because he had trusted in his God (Daniel 6:16-23).

11
ALL THE RIGHT MOVES

by Gene Van Note

On July 2, 1991, President George Bush nominated Appeals Court Justice Clarence Thomas to the United States Supreme Court. A few days earlier, Vice President Dan Quayle had called Senator John Danforth to see if Danforth would shepherd Thomas's nomination through the Senate.

Danforth said yes. It was not a difficult decision for him since he had known and worked with Thomas for 18 years. What the senator from Missouri did not anticipate was that the nomination would be extremely controversial. Nor could Danforth have predicted that he would be nearly consumed by the process to get Clarence Thomas confirmed.

In the quiet luxury of reflection after the bitter but successful battle, Danforth wrote, "I fought dirty in a fight without rules."[1] Danforth's administrative assistant, Rob McDonald, said to his boss, "You were about as far in the gutter as I can ever remember seeing you."[2]

Danforth's actions, public and private, were about what people expect from their elected representatives at this cynical time. People anticipate unethical behavior in the back rooms of government, and are not surprised when they find it—but not from Senator John [Jack] Danforth, who was known in the Senate of the United States as "Saint Jack." Senator Danforth is a man of the highest moral and ethical principles. He is an Episcopal priest and lives his faith. No one in the history of the Senate has ever been held in higher esteem than he.

And yet one of his aides, Ken Duberstein, said after the

Clarence Thomas hearings, "The saint of the senate is far less saintly now than he was four months ago."[3]

What are we to conclude?

Is it true that under pressure the decisions a believer makes and the things he or she does are no different from people who have no faith? That question goes to the heart of this Bible study that leads us to revisit one of the most outstanding men in biblical history—Daniel. So, let's leave our comfortable recliner in front of the roaring fire and go to a place long ago and far away. There we will meet Daniel, a man whose faith in God and faithfulness to God were severely tested.

Daniel and History

Did you ever look carefully at the geographical location of Israel? (All references to Israel will be to ancient Israel, not to the modern nation.)

Israel consisted of a narrow strip of green between the waters of the Mediterranean on the west and the sand of the Arabian desert on the east. It measured less than 50 miles east and west and about 150 miles north and south. A modern jet airplane can fly from Lebanon to Egypt in minutes. An ancient army could march that distance in a week, if not challenged.

Israel had few natural resources but was located in the most strategic spot in the eastern Mediterranean. Except for those who knew where the oases were located and preferred the desert, all north and south traffic in the region went through that narrow strip of land. Egyptian traders and soldiers went north through Israel. Assyrian, Babylonian, and Persian business and military people went south through the same area. The geography of the Near East all but guaranteed that Israel would be a turbulent place. On that count it did not disappoint.

Internal Violence

However, not all the disorder and violence in Israel came from outside. Intrigue, coup d'etat, assassination, and revolt were common. Unwise policies toward the powerful nations of the north and imprudent military alliances brought devastation. Following the death of Solomon, Israel became two nations, or "kingdoms" as they called them back then. The northern kingdom was known as Israel; the southern as Judah. Judah was more righteous, but not much. Israel ceased to be a nation in 722 B.C. Judah continued until 587 B.C. when it, too, was defeated. All its leaders and trained people were taken into exile as the Israelites had been earlier. Daniel, along with others, was taken into captivity in 605 B.C. by Nebuchadnezzar's armies.

Daniel's History

We're not told how old he was when his story begins in Daniel, chapter 1. His exploits do not appear anywhere in the Old Testament outside the book that bears his name. Daniel may have been about 16 years of age when he was forced into exile in Babylon. It is highly likely that Daniel was taken hostage to make sure that Judah's royal family cooperated with the invaders. For most of 70 years, he was a part of the government.

Our review of events in Daniel's life in Babylon will be grouped under these three words, which define the temptations he faced: *collaboration, compromise,* and *tolerance.*

Collaboration

In ancient times, the mass deportation of large population groups for political purposes was common. But this was not a holocaust, such as Hitler's followers visited on helpless Jews. The purpose was not to destroy the conquered peoples but to drain the defeated country of its leadership so it would be easier to govern.

In captivity, the exiles had considerable freedom. In this situation, Nebuchadnezzar ordered a number of handsome, talented, and gifted young men from among the exiles to be trained for leadership roles. Daniel, called Belteshazzar by the Babylonians, and three of his friends were among those chosen. The three were renamed Shadrach, Meshach, and Abednego—of superheated-furnace fame.

Courageously, Daniel asked for a simpler diet than the rich food of the royal table. Ashpenaz, the court official in charge of

the young men, feared what might happen to him if the four Israelites did not look robust when called for inspection. Daniel
asked him to try an experiment for 10 days. He did. The Lord
honored the four so that Daniel and his friends "looked healthier
and better nourished than any of the young men who ate the
royal food" (1:15).

Scholars suggest two reasons why Daniel reacted to the
menu. First, royal food was commonly presented to the gods before it was served. To eat the food was to enter into communion
with the gods. Second, the food was not "kosher," to use a modern term. It was not prepared according to Jewish law; the meat
was not drained of its blood, and so forth. Beyond all that,
Daniel chose not to follow any foreign custom that would make
it appear that he was collaborating with the enemy.

Rarely does a traitor find his or her new life in the adopted
country as optimistic as hoped. Benedict Arnold, a United States
Revolutionary War general who defected to the enemy, was
barred from the British military after the war and despised by the
people in his adopted country. Lord Haw-Haw, an English-lan-
guage broadcaster for Nazi Germany, was convicted of treason
and hanged by the British. Axis Sally, an American and cobroad-
caster with Lord Haw-Haw, was sentenced to 10 to 30 years in
prison and fined $10,000 in March 1949. People who collabo-
rate with the enemy are rarely loved.

However, patriotic reasons were not at the heart of Daniel's
decision. He chose not to cooperate with the enemy because he
would not debase himself before their gods. Others might do
anything for self-preservation and advancement, but not Daniel
and his friends. They would not collaborate with the enemy at
the expense of their faith.

Compromise

"O king, live forever!" (2:4). Kings like to hear those words,
but they didn't satisfy Nebuchadnezzar. He gave his wise men an
impossible task. Tell me what I dreamed and then tell me what
the dream meant, he demanded. "If you do not tell me what my

dream was and interpret it," he threatened, "I will have you cut into pieces and your houses turned into piles of rubble" (v. 5).

When they couldn't (who could!), the king became furious. "He ordered the execution of all the wise men of Babylon. So the decree was issued to put the wise men to death, and men were sent to look for Daniel and his friends to put them to death" (vv. 12-13).

When Daniel learned what had happened, he asked Nebuchadnezzar for an audience. Granted it, Daniel asked for time. I suspect it didn't take much encouragement from Daniel to get his friends to pray for a miracle, prayers the Lord chose to answer. Armed by the Lord, Daniel said to Nebuchadnezzar, "The great God has shown the king what will take place in the future. The dream is true and the interpretation is trustworthy" (v. 45).

Daniel gave the answer and left the result with the king—and God. Nebuchadnezzar was so pleased he made Daniel the ruler of the province of Babylon, and Daniel's prayer partners became provincial administrators. Promotion or not, Daniel would not recognize the king's gods nor bemoan his fate. He would not compromise. The king could demand Daniel's life but could not command his loyalty. Daniel chose to believe that the quality of a person's life is not measured by its length.

Tolerance

We have come to the best known event in Daniel's long life—the lions' den. Told that the king had decreed that no one could pray to any god but the king himself, Daniel did what his enemies expected. He opened his window toward Jerusalem and prayed loudly enough for even his enemies to hear.

A longshoreman from the days when ships were unloaded by hand used to pray in an empty ship's hold at lunchtime. He prayed as loud as he could, hoping his coworkers would hear him and be drawn to the Lord he served. One day a fellow Christian joined him in his "private" devotions. Taken aback by the volume, he tapped the longshoreman on the shoulder and said, "God's not deaf." Whereupon the man replied, "God's not embarrassed either!"

When Daniel was arrested and thrown in with the lions, he

fluffed up the nearest one and, using it as a pillow, went to sleep. In stark contrast, the king was so troubled he rolled and tossed in his bed all night. Daniel understood that there are times when a believer must be intolerant—not to people, whatever their race or national origin—but to the idea that there are other gods. A believer must insist that not all roads lead to heaven.

Many people in our day contend that no one has the right to encourage anyone to change religions. "Proselyte" is the word that is commonly used. Though the dictionary tells us that proselyte means to "convert from one religious belief to another," it has become a dirty word.

Recently the Southern Baptists announced a campaign to reach Jews for Jesus Christ. As a part of that evangelistic outreach they plan to send 100,000 missionaries to Chicago. The *Chicago Tribune* noted that the reaction in Chicago has mirrored the national mood. A group of Christian and Jewish clergy has appealed to the Southern Baptists not to come.[4]

The *Tribune* added, "The Southern Baptists have taken justifiable umbrage at the charge that their campaign may encourage hate crimes. And they have pointed out that their faith obliges them to share the 'good news' with all."[5]

At times a believer must be intolerant. Let's hear it again: *A believer must insist that not all roads lead to heaven.*

What Does All This Mean to Us?

The secular measurement of success is easily defined. Success is upward movement. How you get to the top is not as critical as the fact that you are there, or are moving upward—and doing it quickly. The only reason, in that case, not to crush people on the way up is that you may need them on the way down.

Senator Danforth wrote in response to his administrative assistant's comment, "If Rob McDonald is correct [that he was as far in the gutter as he could remember], . . . then I would have been no more than a politician fighting to save his own skin with whatever weapon was at hand. But I honestly do not believe Rob was correct. I truly believe that I was fighting for a good cause."[6]

Sometimes you win; sometimes you lose. It's that way for everyone—Christian and non-Christian—in the workaday world. Nor is there any reason a Christian should not try to be the best he or she can be.

Senator Danforth has a helpful word here, "Yet to believe in a good cause does not justify using every means to advance that cause. . . . Throughout history, all kinds of atrocities have been committed in the names of causes thought to be good. If there is any lesson to be learned . . . it must be that service of a good cause does not justify the wanton destruction of a person."[7] We would add, not even the *injury* of those who are in the way of our personal advancement.

Does this mean that a Christian is at a disadvantage in the working world?

It seems that way sometimes.

Ultimately, success for the Christian is not measured by positions held or money earned. A final word from Senator Danforth helps us here, "I think it [the Thomas victory] occurred when he acknowledged his weakness and turned to God as the sole source of his strength and his destiny. When [that] prayer is answered, the appropriate answer is, 'Thanks be to God.'"[8]

So we conclude by asking ourselves these three questions:

1. Have there been, or is there now, anything I have done that would compromise my faith?
2. Is there anyone who owns me, someone I have given such unmixed allegiance that they control my future?
3. Have I acted in a way that my coworkers would be surprised if they learned that I am a Christian?

May we, as Daniel was, be enabled to turn to God as our strength and the object of our worship so that we can look back across the years and say, "Thanks be to God."

Notes

1. John C. Danforth, *Resurrection: The Confirmation of Clarence Thomas* (New York: Penguin Books, 1994), 207.
2. Ibid., 161.
3. Ibid., 197.

    4. The *Chicago Tribune* as quoted in the *Kansas City Star*, January 10, 2000, B-7.
    5. Ibid.
    6. *Resurrection*, 206.
    7. Ibid.
    8. Ibid.

About the Author: Gene Van Note is the former executive editor of adult curriculum at the Church of the Nazarene International Center. He is now retired and lives in Overland Park, Kansas.

THE WORLD'S VIEW

To be successful, I must focus on the image I project.

THE BIBLE'S VIEW

True success is Christ-centered.

John the Baptist

In those days John the Baptist came, preaching in the Desert of Judea and saying, "Repent, for the kingdom of heaven is near." This is he who was spoken of through the prophet Isaiah:

"A voice of one calling in the desert,
'Prepare the way for the Lord,
make straight paths for him.'"

John's clothes were made of camel's hair, and he had a leather belt around his waist. His food was locusts and wild honey. People went out to him from Jerusalem and all Judea and the whole region of the Jordan. Confessing their sins, they were baptized by him in the Jordan River.

But when he saw many of the Pharisees and Sadducees coming to where he was baptizing, he said to them: "You brood of vipers! Who warned you to flee from the coming wrath? Produce fruit in keeping with repentance. And do not think you can say to yourselves, 'We have Abraham as our father.' I tell you that out of these stones God can raise up children for Abraham. The ax is already at the root of the trees, and every tree that does not produce good fruit will be cut down and thrown into the fire.

"I baptize you with water for repentance. But after me will come one who is more powerful than I, whose sandals I am not fit to carry. He will baptize you with the Holy Spirit and with fire. His winnowing fork is in his hand, and he will clear his threshing floor, gathering his wheat into the barn and burning up the chaff with unquenchable fire" (Matthew 3:1-12).

As John's disciples were leaving, Jesus began to speak to the crowd about John: "What did you go out into the desert to see? A reed swayed by the wind? If not, what did you go out to see? A man dressed in fine clothes? No, those who wear fine clothes are in kings' palaces. Then what did you go out to see? A prophet? Yes, I tell you, and more than a prophet. This is the one about whom it is written:

"'I will send my messenger ahead of you,
who will prepare your way before you.'

I tell you the truth: Among those born of women there has not risen anyone greater than John the Baptist; yet he who is least in the kingdom of heaven is greater than he" (Matthew 11:7-11).

12

ALL THE RIGHT REASONS

by Donald Demaray

If John the Baptist lived today, he might appear as a curiously odd fellow, walking the hills of his community, dressed shabbily, living rather like a hermit in a hilltop hut, and even keeping bees. He likes honey. Some think him a vegetarian.

Kids make fun of him. When he walks into town, they throw stones at him. Nor do the adults have much respect for him.

That is, they did not until he surprised the townsfolk one Sunday morning in church. This rugged, rough, and ill-clad fellow stood to his feet, walked right up to the platform, and stunned both pastor and people.

A vast quiet stare wrote itself on the faces of the congregation—men, women, and children alike. Everything was silent when John went to the microphone.

He began to speak, his accent John Wayne-like and his speech forthright but eloquent. He cried out against the evils of the people and talked with such convicting power that some began to weep. Others saw themselves as hypocrites (that is, two-faced); still others as feeble believers.

Odd John said more. He cried out against mere traditional religion, ritual as an excuse for genuine experience of God. Some people squirmed in their seats. And well they might, for John called such shallow churchgoers "snakes."

He went on to explain why superficial Christians do not produce fruit—they do not know God's Spirit. John made ever so vivid the truth every Christian knows in his or her heart of hearts, that New Testament religion transforms individuals and groups and whole societies. Real faith sees persons healed of drug addiction, alcoholism, domestic quarrels, gossip, cheating, and so forth. Indeed, Jesus Christ living in hearts means the keeping of all the Ten Commandments and serving, with outgoing love, people in need.

Well, what got through to the people that Sunday morning was that everyone knew John had come from the very presence of God. No longer did they see him as a strange and different man, a hermit from the surrounding hills. They viewed him as one who lived with God. Indeed, they sensed that he dressed the way he did and ate the kind of food he did, not to get attention, but simply because he focused so entirely on God that he did not think much about what to wear or what to eat. People could identify John this way because they detected not the slightest hint of ego. He seemed not to think about himself at all.

"What a remarkable man!" people now said.

Now Some Background

Our little rewriting of the John the Baptist story now requires one or two items of information so we can put him in his own first-century setting. For something like 400 years the Jewish people had no prophet. When John came on the scene, he looked and sounded like a prophet of old. As such, he gladdened the hearts of the common people, and his call to repentance created a desire in them to take steps to put their lives right.

Others like the Pharisees (legalists) and Sadduccees (they believed neither in the resurrection nor in a real heaven) did not like John. Not the least put off, John cried out against their evil beliefs and lifestyles.

Better still, John the Baptist pointed away from himself to the coming Christ. We often call John a "harbinger," one who prepared the way for the coming of Christ. "Harbinger," in its original use, meant someone who went ahead to provide lodgings for a traveler. We think of John as a forerunner, the one who oriented people for the coming of Jesus Christ, Savior of the world.

Herein lies John's goal: to prepare the way for the coming of Christ. And in that he proved himself a complete success.

Commercial Image of Success

If John the Baptist could drop into our 21st century, he would feel ever so foreign to our advertisement-induced, status-conscious mentality. "Image! What's that?" he would ask.

He seemed not to think of himself at all, unless someone asked a question about him personally. Even then, he would point to Jesus.

When the Pharisees gave John a bad time, he went right on with his mission. The Sadducees also ridiculed him; but they simply could not stop John believing in changed lives and holy living. When the Sadducees and the Pharisees confronted John, they ran into a brick wall.

The Pharisees and the Sadducees would like our television ads. They wanted to look sleek, put themselves forward, earn their own salvation. They would have used the "tall, dark, and handsome" rule to choose the King of Israel. But God did not; He chose David, a humble shepherd boy.

The bottom line: God chooses servants He can shape and use. Self-sufficient people rob themselves of God's guidance and help.

For the Christian, humility means surrender to God. That leads to genuine success, success spelled out in heaven's terms.

Where Did John the Baptist Come From?

Well, he came from God himself. Note that he had a message, but not his own. He announced *God's* message to the people.

Yes, he drew crowds, but observe that he did not call attention to himself. He engaged the people in thinking about God.

John got very explicit about his role and Jesus' role. He could only say what heaven gave him to say. He said that he was not the Christ. The climax of all his statements, shifting focus from himself to Christ, comes in John 3:30, "He must become greater; I must become less."

Three Modern John-the-Baptist Stories

Story One: It centers in New York's Bowery Mission summer camp program. Miguel Sanchez, age nine, came to the camp. Today he serves as director of Admissions for Nyack College, a Christian institution of higher learning. Listen to what Miguel says: "Many of my fellow campers have become doctors, lawyers, and professors. What's impressive is that these are minority kids who had no hope before they came to camp."

Some John-the-Baptist type—perhaps not well dressed, perhaps robbing himself or herself of enough food—gave money to send Miguel Sanchez to camp. We do not know who sent the financial aid. God knows. Clearly, the focus was God's mission in the world, not the donor's.

I want to be that kind of John-the-Baptist person. That's success!

Story Two: A bit longer. A poor Methodist preacher in Texas felt a deep need for a revival in his church. When he brought up the idea to the stewards of the church, they told him that the church did not have any money to pay an evangelist. It was 1899 and times were hard in Texas.

The pastor, Rev. Sam Holiday, continued to pray and long for a revival. He was in the habit of going to the barn to pray, where he could be alone in the hay mow. One day as he prayed at his personal hay-strewn altar, God revealed himself. God said, "How about selling your cow to pay the evangelist for this meeting?"

Rev. Holiday balked at the suggestion. "But, Lord," he said, that cow is the source of the supply of milk and butter for my family. How can I spare her?"

God's gentle response was, "Did you not pray for a revival at any cost?"

Rev. Holiday immediately sold the cow for $25.

At the same time the pastor was petitioning God for a revival, his wife had a similar encounter with the Lord. She sold her sewing machine, on which she made all the family's clothes, for $8 and contributed it toward the evangelist's pay.

Because these two saintly people sacrificed, a revival was

held. However, there was only one convert. A teenaged boy was the only new Christian when the revival ended. That was hardly a "successful" payoff for such sacrificial giving, was it?

It doesn't look successful until we look at who the lone convert was. The teenager who knelt at that altar was Roy T. Williams. He rose from that altar to begin a life of Christian servanthood that included being president of a Holiness college, an effective evangelistic preacher, and a general superintendent of the Church of the Nazarene.

That John-the-Baptist pastoral couple had no idea how their sacrifice prepared the way for the spread of the gospel.

Story Three: About a woman who has become legendary, though she always shunned the limelight.

She was given the name Agnes when she was born to poor peasants in eastern Europe in 1910. She received an adequate education and could have done whatever she wanted. But her real love was her Savior, and she desired more than anything to do what He wanted.

She left her home country and opened a home for the poor in a faraway land. For 50 years she did what most people did not want to do. She touched the lives of some of the poorest people on earth in the name of Jesus.

One day she and those with her found four persons, diseased and dying on the streets. They took them to their house to care for them.

Agnes gave the care of three over to her friends, but she took the most sick one as her personal charge. The woman was dreadfully ill and very weak. Agnes put the woman in a bed, which must have been such a relief after lying on the dirty, hard street. Agnes ministered to the pitiful woman as best she could. The woman, though weak, took Agnes's hand and smiled. She said two words—"Thank you"—and died.

Those two words were more than enough for Agnes. She felt the grateful love packed into that short phrase, and it made her Christ-centered life worthwhile.

Who was the woman picked up from the street and allowed

to die in a bed in the presence of one of God's loving servants? We will never know.

Who was the grateful recipient of the dying woman's smile and whispered thanks? We know her as Mother Teresa. The world would not consider her work in the poor streets of Calcutta to be successful by any of their standards. Yet, this small, saintly lady was a John-the-Baptist person preparing the way for the gospel of Jesus Christ to be known all over India and around the world.

The World's View vs. Christ's View

Life does not honor the strut-about person, not even the one who subtly pushes himself or herself forward. The bottom line: the one who loses his or her life for the sake of God's work in the world is the one Christ celebrates.

Imagine! Celebrating John the Baptist. Rugged, unkempt, eating modestly.

His secret? A Christ-centered focus.

Let's face this truth: the world does not gravitate toward those who insist on the personal and moral standards of John the Baptist. The world just doesn't like them. Most of the apostles died martyrs' deaths. Many first-century Christians, refusing to say no to Jesus, died by burning, or by lions who ate them, or by being skinned alive.

In our age of postmodern pluralism (accommodating every moral and spiritual philosophy that comes along), we have lost our sense of absolutes. We have forgotten to recognize truth as truth. We tend to accept the morality of anybody and everybody, no matter what the behavior or the warped thinking.

What will change that? Only the results that come when we put Christ at the center of all the activities and desires of our lives. Only when we focus our existence on the truth that Paul preached about God in Athens: "In him we live and move and have our being" (Acts 17:28).

For disciplined Christians whose hearts are saturated with righteous living, the meaning of Christian success will become clear indeed.

About the Author: Dr. Demaray is professor of biblical preaching at Asbury Theological Seminary, Wilmore, Kentucky. He and his wife are the parents of three children and the grandparents of four.

THE WORLD'S VIEW

The one who dies with the most toys wins.

THE BIBLE'S VIEW

The one who dies with nothing wins.

Jesus

Then the mother of Zebedee's sons came to Jesus with her sons and, kneeling down, asked a favor of him.

"What is it you want?" he asked.

She said, "Grant that one of these two sons of mine may sit at your right and the other at your left in your kingdom."

"You don't know what you are asking," Jesus said to them. "Can you drink the cup I am going to drink?"

"We can," they answered.

Jesus said to them, "You will indeed drink from my cup, but to sit at my right or left is not for me to grant. These places belong to those for whom they have been prepared by my Father."

When the ten heard about this, they were indignant with the two brothers. Jesus called them together and said, "You know that the rulers of the Gentiles lord it over them, and their high officials exercise authority over them. Not so with you. Instead, whoever wants to become great among you must be your servant, and whoever wants to be first must be your slave—just as the Son of Man did not come to be served, but to serve, and to give his life as a ransom for many" (Matthew 20:20-28).

> Your attitude should be the same as that of Christ Jesus:
> Who, being in very nature God,
>   did not consider equality with God something to be grasped,
> but made himself nothing,
>   taking the very nature of a servant,
>   being made in human likeness.
> And being found in appearance as a man,
>   he humbled himself
>   and became obedient to death—
>   even death on a cross!
> Therefore God exalted him to the highest place
>   and gave him the name that is above every name,
> that at the name of Jesus every knee should bow,
>   in heaven and on earth and under the earth,
> and every tongue confess that Jesus Christ is Lord,
>   to the glory of God the Father (Philippians 2:5-11).

Solomon*

I thought in my heart, "Come now, I will test you with pleasure to find out what is good." But that also proved to be meaningless. "Laughter," I said, "is foolish. And what does pleasure accomplish?" I tried cheering myself with wine, and embracing folly—my mind still guiding me with wisdom. I wanted to see what was worthwhile for men to do under heaven during the few days of their lives.

I undertook great projects: I built houses for myself and planted vineyards. I made gardens and parks and planted all kinds of fruit trees in them. I made reservoirs to water groves of flourishing trees. I bought male and female slaves and had other slaves who were born in my house. I also owned more herds and flocks than anyone in Jerusalem before me. I amassed silver and gold for myself, and the treasure of kings and provinces. I acquired men and women singers, and a harem as well—the delights of the heart of man. I became greater by far than anyone in Jerusalem before me. In all this my wisdom stayed with me.

I denied myself nothing my eyes desired;
    I refused my heart no pleasure.
My heart took delight in all my work,
    and this was the reward for all my labor.
Yet when I surveyed all that my hands had done
    and what I had toiled to achieve,
everything was meaningless, a chasing after the wind;
    nothing was gained under the sun (Ecclesiastes 2:1-11).

*We will assume the traditional authorship of Ecclesiastes by Solomon in this chapter.

13

ALL OR NOTHING

by H. Ray Dunning

J esus' ministry is closely related to the entry of the kingdom of God into this world. Both John the Baptist and Jesus began their preaching with the proclamation that the Kingdom was "at hand" (Matthew 4:17, KJV). However, throughout His ministry, there was a tension between the nature of the kingdom He came to inaugurate and the understanding of the kingdom present among the Jews of the day, including His own disciples.

That tension came dramatically to light in Matthew 20:20-28 as Jesus and His followers were traveling to Jerusalem. Using their mother as the intermediary, James and John made a request of Jesus for places of prominence in the Kingdom. Their request reflected a total misunderstanding of the nature of the kingdom Jesus came to inaugurate. We have in this passage a striking contrast between a worldly concept of "kingdom" and the New Testament concept.

Contrasts

Although set in a religious context, Solomon's rise to kingship and the development of his kingdom represent values quite different from the kingdom of God as embodied and taught by Jesus.

If anyone was ever born with a silver spoon in his mouth, it was Solomon. His father David had consolidated the divided nation by gaining the favor of all 12 tribes of Israel, established a royal court and a capital city, and organized the worship at Jerusalem. He entered into treaties with other kings, adopting the practice of having multiple wives, since treaties were sealed in the ancient Near East by the gift of a wife from the king's harem. In a word, David became a typical Oriental monarch, with the one exception that he remained loyal to the worship of the Lord (Yahweh) and insisted that the nation of Israel acknowledge Him as their national God. By the time Solomon was born, David reigned over a wealthy nation, and the king himself was typically rich.

Solomon, born of Bathsheba, was doubtless the apple of David's eye. As was often the case with children of a king, particularly those born from different wives of the harem, there was jealousy and intrigue as David's death approached. Yet, David himself proclaimed that Solomon would sit on the throne in his place (see 1 Kings 1:30).

In order to secure his position, Solomon rather quickly dispensed with his half brother who had been the most active candidate for the throne. He continued eliminating his enemies by having them put to death. Quite a cruel way of establishing his kingdom!

The birth of Jesus could not have been in sharper contrast to that of Solomon. Instead of wealthy, prestigious parents, His were poor peasants, with no social status. Rather than being born in a palace, His birthplace was a cattle stall.

Compromise

The story of Solomon in the Old Testament presents us with an enigma. Initially, he demonstrated some commendable character traits: humbleness, submissiveness to the Lord, eagerness to be a good ruler. When given the option to choose his heart's desire, he asked for wisdom rather than riches or other worldly goods in order to be a wise leader. Scripture records the story of one very positive use of this gift in 1 Kings 3:16-28, which brought him widespread fame. Still, almost from the start, he made decisions and took courses of action that moved him steadily away from the ideal king he seemed to want to be.

In establishing his nation as a nation in the sun, he evidently felt it necessary to enter into treaties with pagan peoples. As previously noted with David, each of these treaties was sealed with the gift of a wife from the king's harem (see 1 Kings 3:1). God had warned against this intermarriage with wives from pagan nations (see 1 Kings 11:2; Deuteronomy 7:3-5).

In deference to the kings and the wives they had given him, Solomon built houses of worship for their gods or goddesses. This compromise resulted in a creeping sickness within the royal court that ultimately issued in Solomon, himself, worshiping these "deities" and abandoning his wholehearted love for the Lord.

One might draw a comparison between this behavior and its consequences and the initiation of Jesus' work to establish His kingdom. At the threshold of His ministry, He was confronted with the temptation to compromise who He was and the nature of His work in order to achieve His goals. In the wilderness, the devil attempted to divert him from the path of suffering that would culminate in the Cross. He offered Jesus the option of becoming a bread-giving Messiah (the temptation to turn stones into bread), to capture a following by spectacular means (jumping off the Temple), or by worshiping Satan himself. But Jesus refused to compromise, even though it led to lack of worldly success, lost Him the multitudes who had followed Him for the loaves and fishes, and culminated with His crucifixion. The real question is: In the long run, which of these courses was the best?

The Temple

The most obvious sign of Solomon's worldly success may be seen in his building projects. The best known of them is the Jerusalem temple. It is important to be aware of two things in order to properly evaluate this undertaking. First, God had initially chosen a simple tent as His dwelling place. It was constructed of quality materials as befitted the majesty of the Lord, but it was not very elaborate.

Second, the Temple was not God's idea. It was David's dream to provide an elaborate house for the Lord. God went along with it but did not initiate it. The building that Solomon constructed was ornate and lavish almost beyond imagination. He hired foreign architects and builders, which in itself introduced alien elements into the structure. Even though God agreed to dwell there conditionally (see 1 Kings 6:11-13), one is left to wonder whether it was not actually more a manifestation of human egoism than divine need. The same question may be asked today about church buildings that are more monuments to human accomplishment than means to advance the kingdom of God.

Jesus himself manifested respect for the Temple of His day but recognized that its proper use had been aborted. Its custodians had turned it into a "den of thieves" rather than a "house of prayer" (Matthew 21:13; also Mark 11:17; Luke 19:46). After His redemptive work was finished, His perceptive followers recognized that God no longer had any use for the temple of stone and other physical materials. Now, God has chosen to dwell in the temple of the human person (see Acts 7:47-50).

Solomon's lust for elaborate buildings then directed its attention toward his own house, a palace. Scripture tells us that it was under construction for 13 years and suggests that it was even finer than God's house, on which Solomon had spent 7 years (1 Kings 6:38—7:1). Scripture further appears to suggest the real motive behind these massive structures: "When Solomon had finished building the house of the LORD and the king's house and *all that Solomon desired to build* . . ." (9:1, NRSV, emphasis added).

The most reprehensible aspect of this whole building enterprise was that Solomon used forced labor from his own people. They were drafted as virtual slaves (see 1 Kings 5:13-16). When the people had initially asked for a king, Samuel had warned the people about the results and predicted that this is precisely what they would experience if they insisted on having a monarch (see 1 Samuel 8:11).

In order to bring delicacies, riches, and exotic goods to his court, Solomon authorized a fleet of trading ships that would go to faraway places. The problem was that the Hebrews were landlubbers and were fearful of the sea. So Solomon hired Phoenician sailors to operate the vessels. The extravagance of Solomon's court as described in 1 Kings is mind-boggling.

Success?

With everything that the eye could enjoy, the taste buds could savor, and the body could experience, it would seem that Solomon would be a success. Yet, in terms of the things that count, Scripture takes pains to demonstrate that everything that he had did not keep him from losing the greatest treasure in the world—a right relation with God. His wives became more than political gifts. He came to worship the gods they brought with them from their pagan homelands. Thus the judgment upon Solomon was that "the LORD became angry with Solomon because his heart had turned away from the LORD, the God of Israel, who had appeared to him twice. Although he had forbidden Solomon to follow other gods, Solomon did not follow the LORD'S command" (1 Kings 11:9-10).

The words of the author of Ecclesiastes capture perfectly the end result of Solomon's accumulation of wealth, popularity, and worldly grandeur:

I denied myself nothing my eyes desired;

I refused my heart no pleasure.

My heart took delight in all my work,

and this was the reward for all my labor.

Yet when I surveyed all that my hands had done

and what I had toiled to achieve,

everything was meaningless, a chasing after the wind;

nothing was gained under the sun (*Ecclesiastes 2:10-11*).

The phrase "under the sun" used throughout this unusual piece of wisdom literature represents a purely secular, this-worldly existence. The absence of a transcendent dimension to life results only in meaninglessness and purposelessness, captured by the term "vanity" in many translations.

Looked at in terms of the standards by which Solomon apparently judged success, Jesus was a miserable failure. He had no palace, in fact He had "no place to lay his head" (Luke 9:58). He was apparently dependent upon others for sustenance of physical life. His court was composed of a small group of rag-tag fishermen, tax collectors, and others of less-than-sophisticated professions. Due to the absence of political power, He was helpless in the face of the ecclesiastical forces of the day and the military might of Rome, or so it seemed. His kingdom was "not of this world" (John 18:36), He claimed. Pomp and ceremony were not its marks, wealth and extravagant display were not important. Like the King himself, the subjects of this Kingdom are servants, not rulers who lord it over their subjects. That was the lesson Jesus attempted to teach His followers in that conversation about the Kingdom on the road to Jerusalem. He later exemplified it for them by taking the towel and washing their feet (see John 13:1-17).

In the light of eternity, which was really the successful life? Anyone with perspective will easily see that Solomon's continual adding up earthly signs of success boiled down to nothing. Yet, Jesus' uninterrupted life of giving himself away ultimately gave Him a "name that is above every name" (Philippians 2:9).

In our day when so many people, even professed Christians, define who they are in terms of what they possess, and life is valued in terms of the accumulation of things even to the point of self-destructive indebtedness, we need to think seriously about the nature of the kingdom of God and seek to live the Kingdom life as embodied in Jesus Christ.

While serving as chairperson of the department of religion at the educational institution where I taught, the public relations department sent around a request to all the department chairpersons. They wanted us to submit a list of names of our graduates who were successful. This is no indictment of the PR folk. If I were the head of the business, science, or music department, I would have had no trouble. Still, what about the religious realm with graduates who had prepared for ministry and gone out to serve God and the church? Sure, there were some who pastored big churches, had become denominational executives, and achieved other kinds of accomplishments. However, I could not judge that the minister who serves a small congregation in a setting where the demographics made significant growth almost impossible was any less successful than those who had achieved high-visibility "success." I did not send in any names because, in God's kingdom, there is a different yardstick by which success is measured. The benchmark is Jesus, not Solomon.

About the Author: Dr. Dunning is retired after serving 14 years as a Nazarene pastor and 31 years as professor of theology at Trevecca Nazarene University in Nashville.